THE
BEHAVIOUR
MANUAL

SAM STRICKLAND

AN EDUCATOR'S GUIDEBOOK

JOHN CATT

First published 2022

by John Catt Educational Ltd,
15 Riduna Park, Station Road,
Melton, Woodbridge IP12 1QT

Tel: +44 (0) 1394 389850
Fax: +44 (0) 1394 386893
Email: enquiries@johncatt.com
Website: www.johncatt.com

ISBN: 978 1 915261 24 3

Set and designed by John Catt Educational Limited

'Put the things you can control in order. Repair what is in disorder, and make what is already good better.'

Jordan Peterson[1]

CONTENTS

INTRODUCTION

INTRODUCTION

**'To create positive behaviour, or not to create positive behaviour...
That is the question!'**

Behaviour is a major school improvement driver. It helps to shape the culture, climate and ethos of a school. It will influence heavily how a school is perceived, viewed and ultimately judged. Behaviour is, for some leaders, the hill to die on or the key to educational success. If you get behaviour right, it will serve as one of your greatest marketing tools. People will want to work at your school. Staff will want to stay at your school. Parents will want their child to join the school where good behaviour is promoted and is an actual living and breathing reality. Behaviour will also support teacher wellbeing and welfare. If you truly want to boost staff morale and support staff workload then make behaviour your first priority. Forget one-hour yoga sessions or staff book clubs and focus in on securing a climate that allows teachers to teach and pupils to learn. If you want academic outcomes to improve, then – guess what? – resolve the climate for learning and prioritise behaviour.

Parents are also very school savvy. Most parents will recognise where behaviour is good and where behaviour is poor. Parental WhatsApp groups are always awash with comments about school behaviour, school rules and the consistency with which standards are, or are not, applied. Ideally you want the parental silent majority to be so large a group that their seemingly quiet support for the school diminishes and dwarfs the very vocal few who do not agree with how your school works.

School improvement plans, while a necessary evil, often forget that the magic – the true magic – happens in the classroom. Generating a climate for learning that allows teachers to truly serve as the experts and affords children an environment where they are able to learn uninterrupted, with every single second of the finite time available and utilised to full effect, is ultimately the halcyon dream we should all aspire to. Yet this magical nirvana of learning and this behavioural oasis is often so hard to achieve, especially in schools in challenging areas or those that rest on their laurels.

Creating a climate of positive behaviour, be it at a whole-school or subject-based level or in the classroom, often perplexes teachers. Behaviour is potentially one of the most controversial and divisive topics within educational circles. It hugely polarises opinion. If we consider behaviour in a political sense, then arguably what we would see plotted is a left–right continuum. Those who believe in rules, routines and, almost controversially, the use of sanctions, are deemed to be on the right-hand side of the continuum. Those that believe in championing pupils, loving the children and listening to them and their needs are often seen as residing on the far left-hand side of this continuum. The debate in some educational circles is borderline binary. However, it is possible, more than possible, to straddle both camps. It is possible to both professionally love the pupils you serve, champion their corner and build incredibly strong relationships with them and, in equal measure, be clear, consistent, strict and use sanctions where appropriate, relevant and proportionate. Educators such as Doug Lemov call this Warm/Strict.[2] Others call it firm but fair. I like both of these terms, but I also like to use the phrase 'children's champion'. That is what an educator is; a champion of the children that they serve.

At times it is essential to be strict. Some see this as a controversial term. However, as an adjective, the term 'strict' means that rules concerning behaviour are both observed and obeyed. I worry when we selectively choose to ignore school rules, be it because we do not like them, do not agree with them or feel we somehow know better. When a member of staff does this in a school, they are undermining an entire school approach. Potentially they are making things more difficult for their colleagues and undermining their efforts. At worst they are saying to the pupils that the school's rules can be ignored. This is a dangerous state of play and can lead to the rise of hero teachers who generate a false sense of secure classroom management.

So, before this introduction turns into a soapbox rant, I hope I have whetted your appetite a little regarding the role that positive behaviour plays. Achieving this is no mean feat and one that ultimately requires lots of hard work, time, effort, thinking, planning and yet more hard work to boot. Generating a culture and climate of positive behaviour is a challenge and a complex beast. There is ultimately no silver bullet.

This book is designed to serve as an educator's guide to behaviour. It is deliberately divided into three clear sections. Section 1 focuses on the role that leaders play at all levels in helping to generate and secure positive behaviour. Section 2 looks at the integral role that middle leaders play and is deliberately pithy. Section 3 examines the role of class teachers, with a multitude of approaches and strategies that teachers can employ to secure a positive classroom culture. Within every section are several spreads that are devoted to an approach or a strategy. In many respects this book has been designed to serve educators in a similar vein and fashion as a Haynes car manual would to a budding automobile enthusiast. You do not need to read this book from cover to cover, though you can. You do not need to read every page, though you may wish to. You may, however, wish to pick a page and read over it or use this book as a referral guide for ideas, advice and guidance. I would strongly recommend leaders at all levels read the entire book. What this book will not do, and this is where I have to be ultimately extremely honest with you, is get pupils to magically behave. But this book may well help you in your quest to create a positive climate for learning, be it at a whole-school level, a middle leader level or within your own classroom setting.

Godspeed.

Key: Please note that in the top right-hand corner of each page is a symbol with either an S or PS. This is to signify if the approach is applicable to secondary (S) or both primary and secondary (PS).

SECTION 1: THE MOTHERSHIP

A GUIDE FOR LEADERS

Teaching should not have to hurt; it should not have to require Herculean efforts to be successful. We need to create a sustainable approach to the job so staff thrive and love what they do and can have a life outside their working environment. If your behaviour systems do not allow the most inexperienced member of staff the platform to teach without their lessons being interrupted or hijacked by behaviour, then your systems are not as robust nor watertight as you think.

INTRODUCTION

'Consistency is fair.' Jenny Fulton[3]

The mothership is the school. You need to visualise the school as a distinct entity in its own right. As a leader, at any level of leadership, you are an evolved member of staff. You are likely to be an experienced school leader, a senior leader, a middle leader or an expert and highly seasoned classroom practitioner. In terms of the hierarchical pyramid, you are in the upper echelons. You are arguably no longer one of the troops; not quite a boot on the ground in terms of endless classroom delivery. Though invariably you will still teach. This does, of course, depend on the phase you are in. Secondary colleagues are likely to teach less as they assume greater responsibility, whereas primary colleagues are more likely to stay in the classroom. The difference between the two tends to be the size of the team they are in charge of. Neither position is easier than the other. However, what is certain is that you are very much part of the decision-making body that makes up the school's leadership structure. You are potentially part of the inner circle of trust as far as the 'boss' is concerned and very much someone who has the inside line.

As part of the mothership you are part of the decision-making body that drives the school. Your actions, decisions, opinions and direction will determine the trajectory of the mothership. As a leader you are essentially the school. When people – be it the children, pupils, parents or community – think of your school, they will think of you and the other experts in your ranks. You embody the school's culture. You represent its ethos, its values, its vision and its mission statement.

If your school's ethos does not resonate with you and your beliefs, then you are in for a testing time as a leader. You will be expected to defend your school to the cliff edge and back at the drop of a hat. You will need to defend decisions that your head makes that you may not agree with. This becomes hugely challenging if fundamentally at your core you do not believe in what your establishment stands for. This is not to sound negative or set this section off on the wrong footing, but this is a hugely important consideration for us all. Our mission alignment is fundamental to our sense of belonging and happiness within the school that we work in.

As a leader, you cannot underestimate the role that you play. It is the Spider-Man adage, where with this privileged position comes great responsibility. This will evoke within you an array of mixed, and at times incredibly contradictory, feelings. There will be times where you feel the position you occupy is enlightening, there will be times when your position will leave you feeling drained and there will absolutely be times where you will feel suffocated by what you have to do.

Within many leadership courses the model of sinking, surfing and swimming is often defined and discussed. Broadly speaking, swimming is where you are just about keeping your head above water, which for many of us is how we will feel day in, day out. Sinking is that horrible feeling where you are below the water surface, where you simply cannot keep up and everything is suffocating. Surfing is the high, where you feel you are on top of your game and nothing at all can stop you. While this will sound bizarre, it is important that you experience all of these states at some stage. If you have never been in the position where you are sinking and fighting the waves, then you will be unable to advise others. Equally, if you are persistently surfing there is a danger that complacency will, quite literally, sink in.

As a leader you operate in a different sphere. If I take each layer of the staffing body, then the new teachers are essentially younglings, the developing teachers are the Padawan learners and you, as a leader, are a Jedi Knight. Everyone will look to you as the established order, as the one who knows everything and as the one who can do everything. Internally you will probably think this crude reference is either crazy or far-fetched.

You will also doubt the relevancy of your established role and the agency of your role in bringing about huge and monumental change. If, however, you pause for a moment and think back to being an NQT, then I want you to consider this; who did you look up to? Invariably it will have been someone from within the established order. An expert teacher or leader who made the job look seamless, who appeared to walk on water, who never appeared to break a sweat, probably in some way, shape or form inspired you or ignited a fire in you that this job was worth the hard work and that, at some stage, you could surf too. This influential position, whether you like it or not, is occupied by you. This is the universe that you reside in. Your position means that you are the ultimate role model for the entire school community.

All leaders should have a backstop. This person is the head. The head should be in a position to guide, coach and mentor you to be a better leader. They should possess the necessary knowledge to adeptly advise you or act as a sounding board. A key piece of advice that I was given as a newly appointed assistant head was that being a senior leader is no longer about you. It is no longer about you doing everything but how you bring out the best in others and how you support them. As a leader you have to navigate a challenging tight rope. On one front you really do need to bring the best out in others, support them and, in many respects, protect them. Then on another front you need to be seen to lead by example. People need to know that you can do the job. While we all want a level of assumed respect from the staff we work with, the reality is you have to earn and maintain their respect. Talking the talk is not sufficient. You have to walk the walk. You need to remember that you should also serve the staff. This applies to all leaders, including the head. Ultimately, the one key area where you will make or break your reputation and gain or lose professional trust with your staff is behaviour and the school's culture. If you fail to get this right staff will cease to follow you. If you secure a positive learning environment where teachers can teach then the world is your oyster. Hence why section 1 of this book has been written and why it is so important for leaders at all levels to ponder how they can help to create a positive culture and support behaviour for the better. Before you engage with this section, there are a number of key questions for you to think about before initiating any change, as follows:

- What are you asking people to do?
- What is the clear rationale underpinning a decision and can you fully justify this?
- Would you do it yourself, assuming you have the ability to?
- Can you actually do it yourself?
- Are you prepared to lead by example?
- What will be the impact of what you are asking?
- What are the unintended consequences of what you are asking?

PS

1: NEW TO LEADERSHIP/HEADSHIP

If you are new to leadership/headship then welcome to the jungle. It is important that you swiftly establish yourself with your school community and become a notable presence/figurehead. It is important to remember a few key points and keep them at the forefront of your mind, as follows:

- Leadership is about how you inspire other people.
- Leadership is about offering certainty and clarity.
- Leadership is about modelling your expectations.
- Leadership is about narrating the how and the why, not just the what.
- Leadership is about being a positive presence that brings about confidence in and from others.

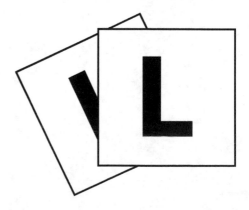

The following flow diagram offers you some ideas of how to establish yourself swiftly and make behaviour a priority:

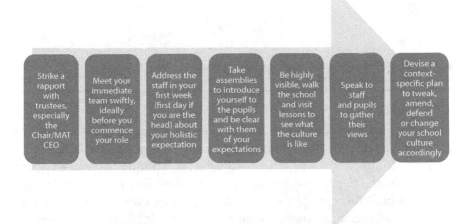

Strike a rapport with trustees, especially the Chair/MAT CEO

Meet your immediate team swiftly, ideally before you commence your role

Address the staff in your first week (first day if you are the head) about your holistic expectation

Take assemblies to introduce yourself to the pupils and be clear with them of your expectations

Be highly visible, walk the school and visit lessons to see what the culture is like

Speak to staff and pupils to gather their views

Devise a context-specific plan to tweak, amend, defend or change your school culture accordingly

WARNING

You must always consider your contextual setting carefully. Trying to railroad an approach without considering your context is at best foolhardy. You should also consider national examples of best practice and how they can be applied to your setting.

ADVICE

I would personally always draw on the following trio to inform my decision making:

- The school's context.
- My own professional expertise and knowledge base.
- Research and evidence.

PS

2: A RESTLESS SCHOOL?

Roy Blatchford wrote a key think piece entitled *The Restless School*.[4] I personally really like this term. If we are truly serious about behaviour, wanting to improve our school culture, continuing to embed our approaches and to improve, improve and improve some more, then I pose the question, 'How restless are we in our pursuit of excellence?' What are we continually seeking to improve, amend and change? I am not suggesting for one moment that we should change for change's sake, nor should we make our changes at 100,000 miles per hour (though sometimes we have to).

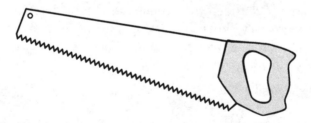

The following key school traits are presented to you to consider carefully how 'restless' you are as a school.

KEY TRAITS TO KEEP YOUR SAW SHARP

Do you regularly review and critique the systems and routines you have in place to ensure that they are highly effective?	Do you draw on localised intelligence to inform your working practices?
Do you empower staff to perform their role effectively, with confidence, and allow them to take risks where appropriate?	Are you outward facing, drawing on examples of best practice from other schools and simultaneously inviting people to visit your school?

WARNING

Never assume you have cracked it with behaviour. The moment you take your foot off the gas and assume that the job is done is the point where things will progressively, and potentially at speed, unpick themselves. It does not take long for a school's culture to unpick itself, but it can take considerable time to rebuild it.

ADVICE

If you get behaviour right in your school, then you are likely to hit something of a frustrating sweet spot. On one front you will have well-established and proactive systems and routines but simultaneously the certainty of these approaches will almost border on becoming boring and metronomic. On another front you will continually assess and critique what you are doing to further embed your approach so it gets stronger with each passing academic year.

PS

3: THE HEADTEACHER

The role of the headteacher is critical and key to the success of any given school. In a school with a deeply entrenched and historically grounded culture, a headteacher is likely to serve as a vanguard of that culture. In a school that is in trouble, a newly appointed head is likely to be afforded almost a blank canvas to drive a new culture, climate and ethos. They serve as an agent of change. Ultimately the head's role is to set, establish and then embed the school's culture, climate, ethos, vision, values and mission statement. Their role is one of setting high expectations and modelling these to the staff. Headteachers are also directly responsible for the systems and standards of behaviour in a school. It is no accident that the headteacher standards identify this as a clear area of responsibility for any given head. It is therefore critically important that a head is the driving force behind designing, crafting and driving a school's behavioural system and behavioural approach. The head should be involved in training both staff and pupils alike and sharing the vision and approach to behaviour with all other key stakeholders. Any head that avoids this is failing in their professional duty.

KEY ACTIONS HEADS SHOULD UNDERTAKE

Heads should immerse themselves in research, speak to stakeholders and visit other schools to gather ideas when creating their vision for behaviour, so the approach taken is evidence informed but also built on experience and the needs of the contextual setting.	Heads should be directly involved in the creation and implementation of any behaviour system that is actioned within a school, otherwise they are not owning the process or are leaving this to less seasoned/experienced staff to design.
Heads should review the behaviour system that is in place to ascertain if it is fit for purpose and teach some lessons to see how the systems work in practice.	Heads should be crystal clear and explicit regarding the standards that they expect to see.

WARNING

A danger for schools is where a head does not involve themselves in designing their school's behaviour system and devolves this to a less experienced member of staff.

ADVICE

All heads should take time to understand, fully, the behaviour system that is in place within their school and then cross-reference this approach against research and nationally heralded best practice (as a starting point) to carefully evaluate if the approach is as strong and sound as it could and should be.

PS

4: WORKING WITH TRUSTEES/MULTI-ACADEMY TRUSTS (MATS)

The role of trustees/MATs is key to the direction of travel and the trajectory of a school's culture, climate, ethos and systems of behaviour. The influence that these respective groups can have is potentially huge. Invariably as a head and a senior leader, you may be presented with a culture that is deeply entrenched, for which your role is to preserve the culture of the school. Equally, you may be operating in a school where you have been given a blank canvas or where you can make tweaks. Operationally, day to day, the head's influence is crucial to the culture of the school. It is anything but amorphous, nor should it be amorphous. I would greatly worry if this were the case and would argue that the head has little influence, direction or a sense of what they want for the school.

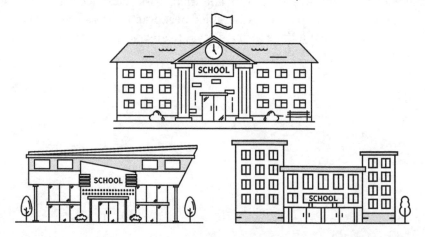

HOW TO WORK WITH TRUSTEES/THE MAT

As with any key stakeholder, it is important to strike up a relationship and to always explain your rationale clearly to them to build and develop their buy-in for any changes that you are looking to make.	Do ensure that trustees/MAT leaders have had the chance to visit your school, to see what behaviour and the culture look like and clearly narrate any changes you are seeking to introduce. Frame this around the question, 'Why?'
Ensure that any key policies you seek to implement have gone through due process and have been signed off by the trustees/MAT so that they are legally binding.	Be open, transparent and measured about the successes and areas for development that you have as a school. Honesty will develop trust and backing for the work that you are trying to achieve.

WARNING

At some stage you will need support with behaviour, for example, a permanent exclusion panel or an Ofsted inspection. You ultimately need trustees and MAT leaders to know how your school-wide systems work, what your processes and rules are, and why those expectations are in place.

ADVICE

You may wish to create a working party to discuss behaviour systems, policies, procedures and training, purely to generate a greater level of awareness and support from a trust/MAT level.

PS

5: SAFEGUARDING

Safeguarding is the number one responsibility of the mothership. If there is nothing else you can do as a school, then at the very least keep the children safe. It is your responsibility to provide staff, governors and pupils with relevant, timely and effective safeguarding training. You should engage your staff with annual Level 1 safeguarding training, ensure you have a number of safeguarding leads who are Level 2 trained, and have a DSL (designated safeguarding lead). It is also best practice to engage in annual Prevent and anti-radicalisation training and to provide your staffing and pupil body with at least a half-termly update that details local and/or national safeguarding matters. At least one member of staff sitting on a recruitment panel should be safer recruitment trained. All staff should be DBS cleared and best practice is to refresh this every five years. Safeguarding can also be a cause of huge frustration for schools, especially given the response rates of some local safeguarding hubs. However, it is key that schools remain vigilant and maintain a culture of 'it could happen here'.

KEY CONSIDERATIONS

Your school must have clear, detailed and precise safeguarding protocols, policies and procedures in place.	Staff must be educated in the four categories of abuse and wider safeguarding matters, with a clear recorded log as evidence that they have engaged in and understood the training.
Have clear and simple systems. Many schools use IT-based platforms to record their safeguarding cases on. Make sure that these platforms do not turn into a two-way email style stream otherwise key concerns can get lost.	Create an annual programme of training as a checklist to work to for any given academic year so nothing is forgotten, and I would recommend undertaking an externally led annual review to ensure your practice is sound.

WARNING

Failing to take safeguarding seriously is detrimental to all parties involved. Ultimately it fails children, it fails staff, and it will cause your school to fail an Ofsted inspection (and rightly so) at the first hurdle.

ADVICE

Ideally, safeguarding referrals should be issued from the member of staff that recorded the referral to the safeguarding lead in person. A hand-to-hand approach is, in my view, far more effective. Schools should also consider organising external supervision and support sessions for those staff who have to deal with safeguarding issues/cases as they can be very traumatic.

PS

6: COVEY'S DEVICES

Stephen Covey[5] devised *The 7 Habits of Highly Effective People.* I often look at these devices when I consider behaviour and how we can have a positive impact on behaviour within our school communities. I personally like to refine Covey's devices into a quadruple of important drivers that can help to support, challenge, change and positively impact on behaviour, as follows:

DRIVERS

Proactivity: Have a clear plan in your mind of what you want behaviour to look like, why, and how to achieve it. Use this clearly defined plan to think carefully about how you can be proactive as opposed to reactive when supporting and dealing with behaviour.	**Prioritisation:** What are your priorities? How many priorities do you have? My own view is to focus on two or three things and do them really well until they become habitual and deeply rooted, as opposed to trying to do lots of things and hoping that something sticks.
Positivity: When considering behaviour it is very easy to slip into a negative frame of mind, to assume the worst and to always see the negatives. This can become all-consuming and, at its worst, paralysing. Flipping the narrative and switching your mindset to focus on the positives is key.	**Personalisation:** Aside from having your systems, routines, vision and values all up and running and embedded, it is important and hugely powerful to keep relationships at the forefront of your thinking. The way in which you are personable, warm and genuinely compassionate towards pupils and staff will help define the culture that you are trying to generate.

WARNING

Do not try and be artificial or formulaic in building your culture and ethos. People, all people, need to see the human side of you. Without this you will struggle to connect with people.

ADVICE

You need to consider carefully the habits and norms that you want to see exhibited in your school community. If you do not know what these are then you cannot expect anyone else to.

PS

7: MISSION STATEMENTS, VISION AND VALUES

Many leadership courses and professional qualifications often start off by getting you to consider your school's mission statement, its value, its ethos and what it ultimately stands for. This can feel verbose, lofty and a bit fluffy. Often you will feel that you are running at 1000 miles per hour as a leader, and thinking about your school's mission statement and ethos will feel like a monumental waste of time. You may well question what difference it will make. The reality though, is if you fail to give your school's values enough consideration, time and thought, then you are likely to come unstuck. If you do not know who and what you are as a school, you are likely to fall short of your aims and strategic vision. You are likely to make decisions and initiate actions that are not in keeping with your school's culture. This is where you can, Grand National style, fall at the first hurdle. Your school's mission statement should be at the heart of all that you do and all that you represent as a leader. A key question to ponder is, 'Are you mission aligned?'

WHAT ARE THESE TERMS? WHAT DO THEY LOOK LIKE? WHY ARE THEY IMPORTANT?

A school's mission statement is a one- or two-sentence summary stating why the school exists. For example, 'At school X, we seek to arm our school community with the knowledge to succeed in the adult world. We want our pupils to strive to be the best version of themselves, mirroring the values of school X's way.'	A school's vision statement usually refers to its future intent. A time frame is often not given as this is an ideal that the school will strive to achieve at an unspecified point in the future. For example, 'School X strives to become a world-class school, offering its community an internationally recognised world-class educational experience.'
Values tend to be key words that define what your school believes in and stands for. These words tend to be virtues or key characteristic traits that you want to promote and nurture. For example, resilience, justice, aspiration, knowledge. Some schools have five or six values. Personally I would have three as this is easier for all stakeholders to remember.	Your school's mission statement, vision and values will ultimately define the type of school you want to be. They should be a touchstone, underpin decision making and, importantly, they should define the type of behaviour and culture that your school stands for.

WARNING

Making your mission statement, vision and values complex, verbose and lofty is a mistake and they won't be remembered or land with your stakeholders.

ADVICE

The mission statement, vision and values should be simple, clear, easy to understand, visible everywhere and become a living and breathing entity that everyone buys into.

PS

8: DEFINING YOUR ETHOS

As I have already shared with you, your school's mission statement, vision and values are important, and these are key documents that you should always come back to. With the same token, so is your ethos. In this section of the book I am simply going to pose seven key questions for you to ponder and write some notes about below. These seven questions are key to helping you to consider your school's ethos, as follows:

1. Do you want to generate a supportive environment where all can thrive? If so, how will you achieve this?

2. Do you want the pupils and the staff to collectively work together?

3. Do you want a school culture built on mutual respect?

4. Do you want a school community that respects the school, the wider community and the locality? If so, how will you achieve this?

5. Do you believe that teachers should shout at pupils?

6. Do you believe in preparing pupils for the adult world? If so, what will you do?

7. Do you want a 'can do' culture in your school, where nothing is impossible?

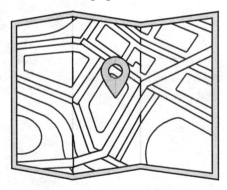

SPACE TO WRITE YOUR CONSIDERATIONS

_____

_____

_____

_____

_____

_____

_____

_____

_____

_____

_____

_____

_____

_____

_____

_____

WARNING

If you do not clearly define and articulate your ethos and expectations then you are simply expecting people to guess what you want. This is where confusion and, at its worst, chaos will occur.

ADVICE

You must take the time to teach your ethos, expectations and behaviour. If you fail to do this, pupils and staff will never truly know what the expectations should look like.

PS

9: STRATEGY

What comes first: culture or strategy? Does strategy eat culture for breakfast or does culture eat strategy for breakfast? This debate is akin to 'What came first, the chicken or the egg?' This is also indicative of so many things within education; namely that as a profession we like to complicate the hell out of things that are actually quite simple, quite straightforward and quite obvious. We like to throw endless academic research at things and make it stick. Please do not think that I am refuting research, its relevancy or its efficacy here. There is a place for research in so much that we do but there is also a place for simplicity, utilising your experience and good old-fashioned common sense. Some of the very best leaders that I have encountered, and indeed worked for, have the ability to take what appear to be highly complex ideas and make them simple and easy to understand. There is no point operating at level X but being unable to translate this into layman's terms. The true craft of teaching and leading is being able to take something that appears difficult and explain it to someone else and make it stick. A school's strategy and culture are no different.

HOW DO YOU KEEP YOUR STRATEGY SIMPLE?

Have a clear five-year plan but unpack this into five one-year plans. Each year you focus on one big thing and one big thing only. But do this proactively and not in response to external data, otherwise it ceases to be strategic.	Keep firmly in mind that leadership is not a race and it can take 12-18 months for changes to embed.
Ensure you communicate your strategy early so stakeholders, especially staff, have time to consider carefully the changes you are looking to employ.	For any one big thing you are seeking to drive, have no more than three underpinning drivers.

WARNING

Be wary of changing your focus every half-term or immediately in response to a change in data or the latest fad. Stay true to what you believe in.

ADVICE

A five-year vision to really drive behaviour could look as follows: **Year 1:** To establish a culture and ethos of success; **Year 2:** To drive pupil attendance for key groups; **Year 3:** To embed systems, processes and routines, with a view that key training will be revisited; **Year 4:** To develop a love and thirst for learning; and **Year 5:** To create success.

PS

10: MOTHERSHIP ROUTINES

The routines that your school holistically has in place say a lot about your leadership, your school, what you value and how you are/are not prepared to operate. They also say a lot about the standards and expectations that you hold dear and how consistent (or otherwise) your staffing body actually is. They are also a reflection of where you have, as a senior team, focused your energy, effort and training. The following key questions have been posed to make you think about the routines you do, or do not, have in place.

KEY QUESTIONS TO CONSIDER

- How do pupils enter your school building at the start of the day?
- How do pupils transition across your school?
- How do pupils enter and leave classrooms?
- What are the routines for learning that you expect teaching staff to employ?
- How do you expect pupils to behave in corridors and communal areas?
- How do you expect pupils to enter and leave assemblies?
- How do you organise lunchtime?
- How do you expect pupils to leave the school at the end of the day?

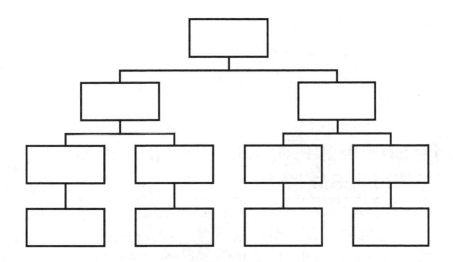

WARNING

It is dangerous to assume that both pupils and staff will simply know how to act in a way that you would expect, especially when you consider the questions outlined above. Taking the view that pupils will just learn how to do it is a naïve one.

ADVICE

You have to continually narrate, train and model the expectations and routines that you wish to see exhibited by both staff and pupils alike.

PS

11: STANDARDS AND EXPECTATIONS: WHAT DO YOU PERMIT?

As a leader and, importantly, as the head, you not only need to define and be explicit about the standards and expectations that you wish to see as part of your school's culture, but you also have to ensure that you are consistent with your approach to enforcing these standards. If, for example, you are insistent that all pupils walk on the left-hand side of the corridor then do you actively ensure that this is the case? What happens when a pupil is walking on the right-hand side? Do you challenge this or let it slide? If you ignore that your expectations, standards and rules have been discarded by a pupil or a group of pupils then you are effectively stating that your rules do not matter and, critically, that they do not matter to you. In this situation, how can you expect staff to enforce something you are not prepared to enforce yourself?

KEY MANTRA

The following key mantra is one to keep firmly at the forefront of your mind regarding your school's rules, expectations, values and norms:

'You permit what you promote and you promote what you permit.'

WARNING

Do not ignore key behaviours that you have clearly stated are unacceptable in your school.

ADVICE

Always ensure, even if you tactically ignore a pupil, that you follow through and challenge a pupil who has not adhered to your expectations.

12: THE IMPORTANCE OF COMMUNICATION

People respond to well-timed, thoroughly thought out and well-communicated approaches. Time is the absolute key. An initiative launched in a Friday staff briefing ready to come into effect on a Monday morning (and I have seen many of these) is often doomed to fail. In making decisions and changes of this nature you have not given people the professional respect of time. It is important to consider that in making a change you are likely to have spent weeks if not months researching, discussing, considering and reviewing your change. A lot of thinking time will have gone into this. However, if you do not afford staff the same level of thinking time then they will not have the same opportunity to consider something in the way that you have. Launching something to come into effect swiftly can be a seductive approach. It may allow you to dodge difficult questions. But it is unlikely to bring people with you. You are unlikely to be seen as the leader or person who is prepared to allow people to engage with you, or that brings openness and transparency to decisions. It is also critical that you carefully consider and constantly communicate your school motto to all key stakeholders so it becomes a habitual part of their vocabulary. Communicating your school's identity until it becomes a collective norm is crucial.

WHY IS COMMUNICATION KEY?

Communication is an area all staff like to critique and criticise.	Effective communication breeds confidence and certainty.
Communicating changes early allows staff the time to think and plan how they will implement the change in a careful and measured manner.	If you want behaviour and a school culture to truly change for the better then you need crystal clear communication.

WARNING

Assuming that people will understand a change and be able to action it with little warning and little training is a mistake and often the change you are trying to initiate will take longer to embed.

ADVICE

When you launch something, allow it to fully percolate in people's minds. Allow them to come back to you with questions and concerns. See those questions and concerns for what they are too. They are not, in most cases, people trying to attack or undermine you. Most of the time those questions and concerns are about people fully understanding what you want and trying to make it work. The motivation behind questioning is often ultimately to support you.

PS

13: COMMUNICATING WITH PARENTS

How you communicate with parents can be vital to the success of your school's culture and how – indeed at times whether – pupils choose to adhere to your rules and expectations. Timely, regular, concise and clear parental communication is critical to ensuring that parents are up to speed with your school's rules and expectations. Through communicating in a regular manner, utilising an array of channels to do so, families cannot argue back that they do not know. It is also important, in the same way that it is with staff, to communicate key changes well in advance of when they are set to take effect from. If there is a change then give families notice and actively encourage and appeal to them for their support.

SOME KEY WAYS TO COMMUNICATE WITH PARENTS

Open weeks in the school day: I would advocate marketing your school to parents in the school day as opposed to in the evening. That way families can physically see what your school is about, and this undermines their ability to argue that they did not know when they challenge you over an approach you have been explicitly clear about.	**A clear, concise and easy to understand home–school agreement that is signed by families and the pupil:** This is a key measure to have in place when a parent chooses to challenge your school's approach.
Explanation videos: I would personally record short and sharp videos detailing elements and aspects of your approach and make these videos easily accessible to families.	**Keep written letters short and precise, with clear and simple language:** It is important to remember that families are busy, have their own jobs/world to consider and will not want to read letters that are 5-6 pages long.

WARNING

Do not assume that because you have sent something out once, all parents will have read and understood your communication. If something is of critical importance, then consider how you communicate home to parents multiple times.

ADVICE

You need to carefully consider the contextual setting of your school to ascertain what the most effective method of communication is that will capture the attention and support of the greatest number of families. You should avoid communicating in a way that you personally feel is effective. Play to your audience, not yourself.

PS

14: HOLDING YOUR NERVE

As a leader or the head, people will challenge you. They will challenge your decisions, approaches, policies and, irrespective of how well you have communicated your stance as a school, someone will find fault and challenge you. I want to share with you a few scenarios where you could easily face challenge and you should take some time to consider what you would do in each of these situations:

Scenario 1: You have communicated your new uniform policy in April in readiness for the new academic year. At the start of the new academic year a pupil has come into school in trainers, which counters your uniform policy. You have isolated them, as per your policy. A parent does not agree and has reported you to the local press.

Scenario 2: A member of staff disagrees fundamentally with your centralised behaviour approach, citing that it is disempowering staff and undermining their professionalism. They are being extremely vocal about this to other members of staff.

Scenario 3: A governor does not agree with your approach to equipping all pupils universally with the stationery that they require to succeed at school, citing that pupils should be independent and purchase their own.

Scenario 4: The local authority has written to you demanding to know why your suspension (fixed-term exclusion) rate is, in their opinion, too high.

Scenario 5: Your local MP has written to you expressing concern over the seemingly strict approaches your school adopts to manage behaviour. The MP would like to know what you are going to do to rectify this matter to appease his constituent.

Scenario 6: The Virtual School feels that your disciplinary response to pupils bringing drugs onto the school site is too fierce and directly challenges you over this, arguing that exclusions do not work and harm the educational life chances of children.

SOLUTIONS

In each of the challenging scenarios that I have presented to you, you will no doubt have had some instant views on what to do and how to respond. The following key points are always worth keeping firmly in your mind before you retort to a situation.

Always remember that your policies will have gone through a process of due diligence, and as long as they have been ratified by your trust board then they are legally binding. I would personally always bounce key policies off my school's legal team to ensure that they are watertight.	Have a clear home–school agreement, which requires families to sign it. If this is in place and a parent has signed that they have read, understood and agreed to the home–school agreement, then their position of attacking you is built on sand.
Unless you are a local authority school, it is worth remembering that the local authority, the local EIPT and the Virtual School have no jurisdiction over you. I would personally invite all of these bodies into your school and narrate to them your approach, coupled with a tour of your school in action. Building a relationship here is important.	Governors, when they are offside, can be challenging. Building a relationship with them and constantly narrating strategic, not operational, matters is key.
If you have a challenging member of staff who disagrees with you or your approach then hear them out. Invite them to meet with you but be very clear what your stance is and unless they have a point that is valid and grounded in fact and research then you may have to be politely clear about the approach the school is taking.	In dealing with the press always have a short, pithy and precise paragraph up your sleeve. Keep any response factual and to the point. Often, if you are being challenged by the media, it is best to keep your powder dry.

Some schools have a strong union presence. Always try and strike up a positive relationship with the union representatives in your school and always take the time to liaise with them.	When you receive a letter from a local MP or councillor challenging your approach, bombard them with information, including the process for creating a policy, that due process was followed, your channels of communication and, importantly, invite them to the school for a meeting. Striking up a rapport, as long as you remain politically neutral, is a powerful move.

WARNING

If you buckle at the first hurdle or the first time someone challenges you over your approach and you change your mind at the drop of a hat, you will never succeed in creating or reinforcing your school's culture. There will always be people who will disagree with you.

ADVICE

Always ensure when you defend your school's approach/stance that you do so from a position of strength and have your collective ducks in a row. Otherwise, a parent will rightly challenge you and make your position difficult.

PS

15: INTERCONNECTED STAFFING APPROACH

It is really important that there is a clear synergy between differing staffing domains within your school setting, to support how student care, behaviour and the school's culture work. If there is a disconnect between any key groups within your school, then you may well find that your holistic approach is undermined or falls flat. It is therefore essential to consider the interconnected relationship between the following groups:

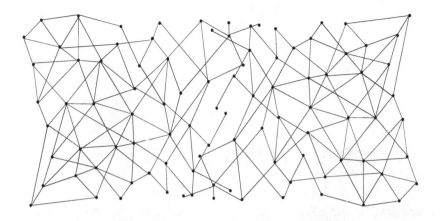

WARNING

You must be clear on the role that you want each group of staff to perform or there will be confusion among staff, which will lead to them citing a lack of institutional communication.

ADVICE

Have a clear set of roles and responsibilities on a clear and simple-to-understand document so staff know what their function is regarding behaviour.

This interconnected relationship between key staff does require some thought, so please use the space below to write down your ideas as to how you want this to work in your setting.

_____

_____

_____

_____

_____

_____

16: HOW MANY SENIOR LEADERS?

Many schools will have a senior leader who serves as the behaviour lead. Their role is invariably vast, with responsibility for behaviour, attendance, safeguarding, a team of tutors, a team of year/house leads, pastoral staff, parental engagement, standards, assemblies, PSHE, tutor time, etc., etc. I have served such a role as a leader in the past. The reality is that the role is overwhelmingly vast. Yes, it serves as incredible professional development and you do learn an awful lot in such a role. But when we pause and consider what is being asked of this person, the actual to-do list is insurmountable. It is beyond vast. Any one given safeguarding matter can take you out of circulation for half a day. A meeting to review the progress of a child in looked-after care can take two to three hours.

Often this solo Batman-style leader is the focal point for everyone as ultimately behaviour is a major part of any school's curriculum and culture. They are the go-to for all issues. They are the person parents will gravitate to, likewise staff and pupils. If you are in any doubt about how vast their role is, then take a look at the number of emails they will receive in any given day. It is not a sustainable role. There should, in my view, be a collective senior team approach. There should be multiple senior leaders involved with driving behaviour, standards and expectations. In truth, every senior leader within a senior team should be responsible for behaviour. It is naïve to think that other staff will always support this person when they have to juggle their own role and remit, for which they are accountable. It is also worth noting that primary leadership teams tend to be smaller in size than secondary, but the same joined-up thinking should still apply.

SOLUTIONS

Think carefully about your school setting, and the size and composition of your senior team.	Make behaviour the senior team's responsibility. It should be the responsibility of the collective and not the individual. All leaders should be accountable for the culture and standards within a school.
The head cannot and should not be dislocated from the school's behaviour system.	Each leader should have a clear and discernible aspect of behaviour that they are driving to ensure accountability.

WARNING

Do not assume your senior team will automatically know how to lead on behaviour. They, like any other staff group, will need training, support and guidance. This should come from the head.

ADVICE

Think of the senior team as a collective, with clear lines of responsibility and accountability for leading on key aspects of the school's behavioural approach, *but* also consider how the senior team can and should drive behaviour as a unit.

17: VISIBLE LEADERS

What exactly does the term 'visible leaders' mean? At its simplest, it means leaders who are ever-present, who walk the school, who can be seen and who publicly serve. They act as vanguards of the school's culture, ethos and expectations. They are on duty in the morning to welcome the pupils into the school, they walk the corridors during lessons and go in and out of classes to check with staff that everything is to their satisfaction and equally interact with the pupils. They are present at break/lunch, they head up assemblies, they conduct line-ups and they are present at the end of the school day to say farewell to the school community and wish them a good evening. The concept of visible leaders seems a really simple one and one that requires minimal consideration and thought. However, it actually requires a lot of careful consideration and planning.

SOME KEY CONSIDERATIONS

You need to have a set of leadership expectations, akin to a list of dos and don'ts. This will set the tone for what you are about as a leadership team and how you will set about your business as a collective.	If you are going to be truly, constantly and consistently visible as a leadership team then you need a rota. Each member of the team cannot yomp the corridors all day every day, otherwise nothing else would get done.
Consider carefully what goes. If leaders are going to be visible for approximately two hours a day each on average, depending on the size of your team, then you need to carefully consider what work needs to be parked, omitted or deemed irrelevant. You cannot do it all.	Define carefully what visible is for you. Visible, if you get it wrong, can be perceived by the staff as you spying on them. You do not want to generate this sort of culture, which turns into one of fear and suffocation.

WARNING

Where leaders fail to be positively present and visible, staff quickly lose faith and confidence in the levels of support that they receive. There is a real psychology to this. If staff feel unsupported then morale will nosedive.

ADVICE

Firstly, not all routine line management meetings have to take place behind closed doors. You can walk and talk, which can be more productive. Secondly, if you know your team is going to be behind closed doors for a day (for example, you are conducting interviews) make staff aware in advance. Staff are more likely to respect you for being honest.

18: RED LINES

Red lines are often referred to as 'non-negotiables' or 'lines in the sand'. They are ultimately the behaviours that you are not prepared to condone or allow in your school setting. To some they will sound like zero tolerance and to others having red lines will sound sensible. This is a divisive topic and one that polarises opinion. Arguably everyone has a set of behaviours that they are not willing to allow, tolerate or condone. The question is, what do you do about these behaviours when they occur? I do believe that schools need to employ the use of both suspensions (fixed-term exclusions) and permanent exclusions. There is a need to keep schools and the people working within schools safe.

Where would you stand if a member of staff was sworn at? How would you deal with a pupil creating videos of staff members and publishing them live online? How would you deal with a pupil who has deliberately assaulted another pupil or member of staff and broken a bone in their body? I appreciate that these examples sound extreme, but they do happen and they do warrant a response. Failing to respond to these issues proportionately is to fail your professional duty. It is also worth considering that permanent exclusion was never designed to be the end. Local authorities are responsible for placing a permanently excluded pupil into another school setting if appropriate and/or providing them with alternative educational provision. It is also important that when a pupil is suspended they use the time away from school to not only keep up to speed with their academic studies, but to also reflect on their actions, why they have been suspended and to contemplate how to move forwards. These considerations should form the basis of any given reintegration meeting.

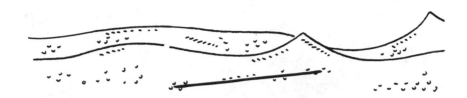

KEY POINTS TO CONSIDER

Think about which behaviours you feel would warrant either a suspension or a permanent exclusion and make a list.	Always consider the necessity and the need to keep your school community safe.
Once you issue a suspension you need to consider the 'what next?' question. How will you support the pupil in question to avoid them becoming a repeat offender?	If you are going to have lines in the sand then you need to carefully communicate these to all key stakeholders and have a clear policy that underpins your approach.

WARNING

If you have a set of lines in the sand but never actually suspend or exclude a pupil who breaks them, then what message does this send out to the rest of your school community?

ADVICE

When deciding to suspend/exclude a pupil it is important that a full investigation has taken place, with witness statements gathered from everyone involved. A pupil may be going through troubling circumstances but that does not mean that they should not be suspended. This contextual consideration may influence the length of the exclusion.

PS

19: SCHOOL RULES: YES OR NO?

Every school should have a clear, discernible and easily understood set of rules. If we step for a moment into the world of politics, the general rule of thumb around sound bites and messaging is to stick to the rule of three. In other words, you should have three key messages that are clear, succinct, memorable and easy to grasp. School rules are crudely put quite similarly. They need to be easy to understand and remember. I have seen schools with rules that go on for pages and pages and pages. An important question to ask yourself, when considering what your rules are, is will the youngest child in your school know what they are and be able to remember them? If the answer to this is no, then you need to start again. School rules are ultimately essential as they represent the standard you are willing to accept, they outline what your school is about and they should focus the mind on what the purpose of the school is. Your rules should also neatly dovetail with your school's mission statement, vision and values. They should align with the school's ethos and will define your school's culture.

YES/NO

SOME THOUGHTS

One rule should home in on the role of the teacher as the expert and the need for pupils to listen to and respect staff.	One rule should focus on being ready to learn. This emphasises the importance of learning, which is ultimately why children come to school.
Your school rules should be clearly visible in every classroom in the school but, in equal measure, should be a living and breathing entity and not just some words on a page.	The consistency of how your school rules are adhered to and applied will determine how strong your school's culture ultimately is.

WARNING

Try to avoid ambiguity with the language that you employ when devising your school rules. For example, if you want pupils to be silent when a teacher is talking then make that explicitly clear. Do not have a rule stating pupils should be 'quiet' when a teacher is speaking. My definition and your definition of quiet could be very different.

ADVICE

Think carefully about the point and the purpose of your school rules and always be able to narrate why they are there. If you are unable to verbally justify them then you will need to reconsider the rules that you have in place.

PS

20: HOW MANY WARNINGS?

The behaviour system that you create and use as a school will be fundamental to how successful every element of your school improvement plan ultimately is. If the system you have in place is garbled, confusing, cumbersome and difficult to navigate, then staff will give up on it. If there is no support, or continually a sense that staff are negatively challenged over how they have dealt with a behavioural issue, then they will give up. The system that you have in place has to support staff so they can perform their core role and not be detracted from it. A key consideration for any senior team is to decide how many warnings they feel are appropriate when devising and driving a behaviour system. In equal measure, you should always consider the unintended consequences of your behaviour system and where pupils are likely to pick holes in it.

SOME KEY THOUGHTS

- How many warnings do you want to have in place?
- If you have three warnings, which is a fairly common approach, then what happens when a teacher has a challenging class and is issuing up to 90 warnings in a lesson (based on a class of 30 pupils)?
- How sustainable is the warning system you have in place in terms of teacher workload, and their ability to deliver their lessons and perform their job?
- Are pupils able to get away with certain behaviours because the system you have in place does not tackle their behaviour effectively?

- Is the system age and stage appropriate, which is critical in a primary setting?

WARNING

If you have a behaviour system that is built upon multiple warnings before a consequence is issued, then it is possible that your school could have a culture of low-level disruption and white noise in lessons.

ADVICE

When devising or revising your warning/behaviour system, speak to the older pupils within the school and ask them for their honest views. Pupils will be able to pick a fault in any behavioural approach if they see one and will give you the pupil perspective as to where the pitfalls in your approach reside.

PS

21: MOBILE PHONES

School approaches and views on the use of mobile devices can vary. In some quarters the view is that a school should allow their use, that they are an aid to learning and that it is our job as the professionals to educate the children we serve in how to use them safely and effectively. Other people take the view that they are a distraction to learning and create more issues than they resolve. I am sure, especially in a world of remote education, that technology can serve a purpose, but I personally do not agree with pupils using phones in school and question the positive impact that they have on pupil learning.

POINTS TO CONSIDER

You need to have a clear policy and approach on mobile devices.	If you are going to allow mobile phone use, for example during communal times, then you also need to be prepared to accept responsibility as a school for any issues or unintended consequences that arise as a result.
If you are going to ban mobile devices you need to consider what the consequence will be for any infringements.	Invariably parents will challenge you regardless of your position and approach. You must be able to credibly defend your stance and stand firm.

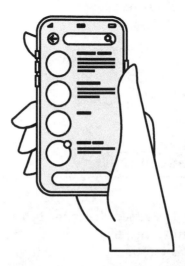

WARNING

Irrespective of whether your school allows mobile devices to be used or not, it is essential and critical that you still teach your school community e-safety.

ADVICE

I would recommend walking in the shoes of a school safeguarding lead for a week to see the volume and array of issues that they face before considering whether to allow pupils to use phones in school.

PS

22: THE SOCIAL NORM

In some quarters, it is claimed that poor behavioural decisions are a form of communication and that they are a manifestation of unmet needs. Sometimes this can be the case and it would be remiss to deny that communication and unmet needs do not exist. However, what can be forgotten is that at times children are, by and large, conformist in their nature. Their actions are often a representation of the social norm engineered by the behaviours exhibited by their peers, by their families, by the environment that surrounds them, by the school and by what a school both permits and promotes. Sometimes children like to test the water and push the boundaries. Some children do this simply because they can or because they choose to. Some do it because they are bored. Some do it because they struggle to access the curriculum. Some seek to follow their peers or impress their classmates. Why do they do this? Because 'to err is human'. Children make mistakes. They have not fully formed as people and often do not see the ramifications of their actions or realise the impact that they are having on other people. In a school setting this is more likely to happen where there is a lack of certainty, consistency, routine and clearly discernible rules. The challenge for any school is to therefore flip the narrative and make it 'cool to behave', to reward (appropriately and proportionately) pupil achievements and to publicly celebrate the successes of children.

HOW CAN YOU CHANGE THE SOCIAL NORM?

Having sky-high expectations is a clear starting point but these need to be narrated daily to both staff and pupils alike.	Create a healthy sense of community and competition among the pupils, which can often be generated through a house system, school-based charities and opportunities to bring groups of pupils together.
Have a clear, consistent, explicit and easy to understand set of rules that have been overly communicated, with pupils and staff continuously trained in them so that they become habitual.	Constantly platform pupil successes and achievements and reward those successes so the silent majority are recognised publicly by the school.

WARNING

Underestimating the importance of the social norm can seriously undermine a school and the culture it is trying to achieve. Do not leave this to chance.

ADVICE

Do not ignore the silent majority and do not allow the social norm in your school to leave these children disaffected and disillusioned. Work swiftly to bring these pupils on board with the culture you are seeking to generate, otherwise you risk losing your school.

PS

23: PROMOTING CHARACTER

Character, succinctly put, encompasses the virtues and values that you want your school community to be immersed in. It is the gold standard of ethical disposition that you want your pupils to demonstrate at all times. If you develop character effectively then behaviour in your school community will dramatically improve. You will inspire pupils to behave not because they have to or are told to but because they have consciously chosen to do so. Many schools have considered how to deliver character education to their pupils. I think it is important to carefully consider that the development and education of character should come through all aspects of your school's approach and curriculum. It should be entwined in all that you do as part of your school's distinct way of doing things. Character should not become a bolt-on that a school tips its hat to.

POINTS TO CONSIDER

Do you have a clearly defined identity as a school? One that encapsulates who you are, what you believe in, what your moral purpose is? Is this understood by all key stakeholders and can they articulate this?	Are the values of your school lived and breathed within the curriculum and your curriculum delivery?
Are there clear artefacts throughout your school that promote the development of character?	To what extent have you truly critiqued how your curriculum, ethos, culture, values, behaviour and pastoral systems all interlink and talk to one another?

WARNING

Do not view the development of character as an artificial bolt-on to your curriculum design.

ADVICE

The head has to live, breathe and be passionate about the development of character within the school, otherwise promoting character will fall flat. Everything starts from the top.

PS

24: MAKING SMALL STUFF A BIG DEAL

Sweating the small stuff is really important. If you make small things a priority then pupils and staff will know that they matter. They will also know that behaviour is taken seriously. For example, if you are pushing the same three things over and over and over as a school then stakeholders know that this is a real focus. Pupils begin to realise that if they are going to be challenged and have their behaviour redirected over what appear to be small and seemingly trivial matters, then the school is clearly not going to condone nor tolerate bigger infringements.

HOW CAN YOU MAKE THE SMALL STUFF A BIG DEAL?

Have a weekly rota on repeat for the main area you are really going to home in on. For example: week 1 – uniform, week 2 – punctuality, week 3 – manners. In a primary you may shift the focus to: week 1 – turn taking, week 2 – playing kindly, week 3 – being polite.	Ensure that you repeat the weekly rota every three weeks so the focus never detracts from the core areas you are trying to drive.
Ensure staff are made aware of the weekly focus, with the rota ideally displayed across the school.	Ensure that your messaging to the pupils is clear and the meaning transparent.

WARNING

If you are truly going to sweat the small stuff then you have to make it a priority and never assume that it will just happen. This needs to be more than just one briefing a term reminding staff of the key areas to focus on.

ADVICE

Senior and pastoral/middle leaders will need to be highly visible and lead by example if you are truly going to sweat the small stuff. This is where class teachers will need to be supported and backed up if they are to become confident and consistent enough to successfully challenge pupils.

25: CENTRALISED OR DECENTRALISED BEHAVIOUR SYSTEMS?

Having a behaviour system that is centralised and therefore in the direct control of the mothership versus a decentralised behaviour system that is left in the hands of the satellites that make up a school (often subject teams) is a topic that can become hotly contested. My view is that this is a no-brainer. The mothership should and has to take control and direct how the behaviour system works in a centralised manner. If we go back to the headteacher standards then how do you truly know as a head and a leadership team what is going on in your school if the behaviour system is not centralised? How will you deal with issues as they arise and know about them in real time? How will you detect patterns, trends and themes if you do not centralise your approach? Of equal importance, how will you support your staff fully if you leave behaviour to chance? Some will argue that a decentralised system of behaviour empowers staff to deal with their own issues and the behavioural matters that arise in their classes. Personally I feel that this is, at worst, a lazy narrative. An important point to consider is what do you actually want staff to focus on? Behaviour management and chasing up behavioural issues, or the curriculum, subject knowledge and how the curriculum is enacted? The reality, given the finite time we all have in school, is that teaching staff and heads of subject cannot do both. So if you are not prepared to centralise and take ownership, which I believe is a huge mistake, then you need to consider carefully what you are prepared to compromise and the consequences of this. A centralised approach can work in both a primary and a secondary setting.

HOW DOES A CENTRALISED APPROACH WORK?

Firstly, the behavioural rules, processes and procedures for the school should be directed by the mothership and cascaded to staff.	The manning of punitive sanctions (for example, detentions) should be conducted by senior staff in the school and not by teaching staff and heads of subject. These should be held in clearly defined areas of the school.
Sanctions should be progressively increased in a clear and systematic manner to reflect the poor behavioural choices made by pupils.	There should be clear follow-through and communication with home when a pupil ends up being issued with a punitive sanction.

WARNING

A dangerous narrative is that teaching staff become professionally de-skilled if they are unable to deal with negative behaviour themselves under a centralised system. This is a false narrative. Teachers still have to be able to exercise sound classroom management, but they are safe in the knowledge that the school will not only back them up but, critically, support them.

ADVICE

It is important that you keep any centralised system simple. When positioning detentions consider what time of the day works best for your school setting and how pupils travel home at the end of the day. Consider also the level of follow-through and backup that your centralised system will employ.

A key question to consider: do you really want teachers chasing pupils for weeks on end to serve a detention?

S

26: ON-CALL SYSTEMS

Having an on-call system, especially in a larger school, is often a very good idea. It helps staff to feel supported. It demonstrates that senior leaders (assuming they are the staff on call) are visible, bothered and they care. It reinforces to the pupils that the school takes learning, teaching, its rules and expectations seriously. I appreciate I am talking more positively about on-call systems here. There are of course potential issues and problems attached to such systems and indeed unintended consequences to such an approach.

POINTS TO CONSIDER

Who will patrol the school and be part of the on-call system? Senior leaders? Pastoral leads? Subject leaders?	What work will you remove from the staff who are on-call to ensure that they are free to patrol the school?
How will staff alert the on-call team? How practical and easy is the approach?	What do staff do once they arrive at a lesson where there is an issue? What is the process and procedure?

WARNING

You should trial actioning your on-call system and ask staff for honest feedback. Is the system you have in place simple enough? If a staff member has to write an email, for example, then how practical or appropriate is this if the situation at hand is challenging?

ADVICE

If a member of staff has requested on-call then it is likely that they need support. That staff member will not need challenging over why they have asked for support in that particular moment. They will need you to assist them with the removal of the pupil from their class. You can always ascertain what happened and what led to the pupils needing to be removed afterwards, but never do this in front of the class and never undermine the teacher.

S

27: ISOLATION/REMOVAL FROM CLASS

There is a lot of debate – in some quarters, highly heated debate – over how isolation is used. There are those who cite that isolation should never happen and argue that isolation rooms are fundamentally wrong, whereas at the other end of the scale there are those who firmly believe that isolation rooms are key to how their school operates. My objective starting point with isolation is this: when and why would you remove a pupil from a lesson? If you cannot answer this question, then perhaps isolation will not work for you. It is sensible to consider key scenarios which could play out in your school that would lead to the need for isolation. Over the course of my career I am yet to actually see an isolation room work effectively. My fear is that you are always, inevitably, putting some of the most challenging pupils across your school together in the same room with one or two members of staff. There are two dangers to my mind. 1) That younger pupils will learn negative behaviours from older pupils. 2) That you need really strong staff to make these rooms truly work. That is not to say that some schools do not successfully operate isolation rooms; they do. My own method, and I would argue that this works effectively, is to isolate pupils with a pastoral or senior leader in their office.

HOW CAN ISOLATION WORK?

You need to have a clear on-call system within your school, whereby if staff need to remove a pupil someone will come swiftly.	Once a member of pastoral or senior staff arrives to remove a pupil, they should ask the member of staff what has happened and judge whether the pupil needs removing for the lesson or for the day. It may be that the behaviour warrants a suspension or exclusion.
Members of staff should never be undermined. If a member of staff needs a pupil removing in that moment and you contest this then you have publicly undermined that staff member to the class.	The pupil should be isolated with a pastoral or senior leader, with a view that they will work in their office for that lesson/the day and have their break/lunch with that member of staff.

WARNING

As a pastoral/senior leader you may have a confidential meeting or have to teach on any given day that a pupil is isolated with you. You need to create a system for ensuring that the pupil is not forgotten and either safely handed to another member of staff or comes to your lesson.

ADVICE

Always ensure that the pupil in question has work to do, that they are not sat idly doing nothing and also ensure that you take the time to address why they have been removed from the lesson.

PS

28: HATE AND BULLYING

There is a real criticism of zero tolerance approaches in some quarters, citing such approaches as inflexible. However, I would argue that everyone has a form of zero tolerance towards certain behaviours that they object to. We all have an inbuilt level of tolerance, or lack of. However you want to paint hate infringements and acts of bullying in schools, they have to be dealt with seriously and proportionately. In many regards there is a zero tolerance towards these behaviours. All hate incidences have to be logged and reported; there are no exceptions to this rule. While many hate issues can be dealt with by the school, occasionally some have to be referred to the police. Bullying can have a huge detrimental impact on the mental wellbeing and mental health of the child on the receiving end. I have seen some incidences of bullying turn into safeguarding issues within my career.

CONSIDERATIONS

You must have a clear approach to bullying and ideally an anti-bullying policy; likewise for hate incidences.	Your curriculum should detail clearly when and how you will educate pupils in hate crimes and anti-bullying.
You need to be clear on the sanction/s that a hate or bullying incident will carry, and educate your pupils fully about actions and consequences.	You should consider carefully how you respond to issues that arise as a school. For example, do you follow up on incidents with a clear approach to educating pupils about the issues that have arisen?

WARNING

Children make mistakes. Sometimes a child may say something naïvely to another pupil without fully knowing what it actually means. You will still have to record the hate incident but you should consider carefully how you educate the child in question, so as not to have a repeat of the behaviour.

ADVICE

Whenever a hate incident or an act of bullying occurs, keep your safeguarding hat firmly on. This is not to excuse the poor behavioural choice, but there could be a deeper safeguarding issue at play.

S

29: RESTORATIVE JUSTICE

Within the circles of behavioural educators, the employment and use of restorative justice as a tool for redirecting behaviour is perhaps one of the most divisive. The key principle that restorative justice is built upon is a sense that the harm caused by a misbehaviour can be repaired, but through a co-operative process where all of the stakeholders involved meet to discuss the issue at hand and devise a solution to positively move forwards. This approach has come from the prison system and is advocated by a number of leading educational consultants.

Restorative justice can play a role in redirecting pupil behaviour. Some schools utilise this tool as their main modus operandi to tackle and address negative behaviours. There are pitfalls to this approach being *the* approach within a school. Most notably, staff can feel disempowered, pupils can realise that over time they are unlikely to be sanctioned for their poor behaviour and it can lead to resentment among those pupils/staff who are on the receiving end of negative behaviours. There is also a need to respect that some pupils will not want to sit down and discuss why, for example, someone has bullied them, and that some staff would not want to sit and speak with a pupil who has assaulted or abused them.

POINTS TO CONSIDER

Restorative practices should only be actioned by key senior staff who have received specific and extensive training in how to effectively carry this approach out. It should not be a universally held approach for resolving all issues across all staff.	The pupil in question who has infringed upon the school rule should still be issued a punitive sanction and serve this first.
You should check, and genuinely check, that all relevant stakeholders are prepared to discuss the matter sensibly.	Staff should never be left to feel that they are undermined or somehow at fault for having upheld the school's expectations in a professional manner.

WARNING

Restorative approaches can work well if used carefully and in a considered manner. Where they become the main method of dealing with misbehaviour it is possible that teachers will end up negotiating and almost bartering with some pupils to get them to behave. This can create resentment and negatively impact staff morale.

ADVICE

Do consider where restorative practices could be employed as part of a wider holistic approach. They can add another dimension when trying to redirect pupil behaviour but this approach should be used sparingly.

30: HOUSE SYSTEMS

Some schools have house systems in place. This is where you divide your school community, staff and pupils alike, into one of three to six houses (depending on the size of your school). Pupils from all year groups make up any given house. Therefore, they are vertical in composition and staff from an array of differing areas of the school belong to any given house as well. Often schools will have a head of house and potentially a senior leader attached to each house. My own view is that you should be clear about the role and remit of the house. In other words, is the function of the house to generate a positive sense of community, is it to serve as a pastoral vehicle, or both?

SOME KEY CONSIDERATIONS

House names: What do you call the houses? It can often be very powerful for the pupils to come up with these themselves.	**House mottos:** It is often wise that each house has its own motto, which will help to craft the identity of the house and can be referred to, for example, in assemblies.
House badges: You should ideally base these around the house name but house badges, worn by staff and pupils, help to generate a sense of identity and community.	**House charities:** Having a house charity can be a powerful way to create a collegiate identity and sense of wider community purpose.

WARNING

Personally I would not confuse nor blur the role that a house plays. If a house system infringes on the role that heads of subject, phase leads or heads of year play, then you could potentially create confusion across the school regarding the systems you have in place.

ADVICE

If you are going to create a house system as a school, then you need to platform it and ensure that it is given the kudos that it deserves.

31: PUPIL LEADERSHIP OPPORTUNITIES

How do you empower pupils to take the lead in your school? What sort of pupil leadership positions do you have available? How do you utilise older pupils to mentor and support pupils lower down the school? It is easy to assume that pupils cannot contribute to the culture and fabric of a school and it is equally all too easy to be dismissive of what children can bring to the table to help drive your school culture.

SOME SOLUTIONS

Prefects: Having a clear interview process where pupils are appointed as prefects is a fantastic way of developing pupil voice.	**Student council:** There are often many pupils who would relish the chance to form a council, to meet with staff and the head to give their perspective as to how a school can improve.
Litter monitors: Some pupils relish in this opportunity. They will actively support in the picking up of litter and, rightly, deserve to rewarded for their support.	**Head student team:** This is where a collective of older pupils can be pulled together into a team and can be called upon to represent the school at open events, key talks, touring people around the school, interviews etc.
Peer mentors: Older pupils can help to support pupils in younger years with their learning.	**Bullying mentors:** Responsible pupils can be called upon to support pupils, from a pupil-to-pupil perspective to discuss times when they have been bullied.

WARNING

Do not ignore the power of pupil voice and what pupils can ultimately offer. The pupils of your school are one of the most loyal and dedicated set of advocates for their school community.

ADVICE

For any pupil leadership position that you create, ensure that there is an interview process in place. Do not turn it into a beauty pageant-style extravaganza where pupils ultimately vote for the most popular pupil.

PS

32: MANNERS/BECAUSE WE CARE

How we speak to the children we educate is hugely important. The modelling we demonstrate to our pupils is critical. As I have stated in other sections of this book, children are conformist. If they are educated in an environment where manners, courtesy, care, warmth and respect are lived and breathed, then the chances are that they will emulate these behaviours too, and they will become part of the established institutional social norm. How we narrate manners is critically important to children, and not just the how, but also the why.

SOME EXAMPLES

1: It is polite to ask teachers how they are and to say good morning/good afternoon to them. It is also polite to respond to teachers when they say good morning/afternoon and ask 'How are you?'

Why? It sets a warm and friendly tone. These are basic manners and form part of our normal etiquette.

2: We should speak to one another clearly, articulately and without grunting, moaning or placing our hands over our mouths.

Why? We are trying to engage with one another in an adult manner, showing each other positivity and carrying ourselves with confidence. Imagine how you would feel if your teacher was rude and dismissive towards you.

3: We should remember to use 'please' and 'thank you'.

Why? These are important basic manners that will speak volumes about you as a person.

WARNING

If you cannot explain adeptly why you want the manners you expect to see demonstrated, then you have not carefully considered them. If the staff do not model the expectations that you have set out as basic norms, then you will struggle to get your pupil body to adopt them.

ADVICE

Demonstrating to pupils every single day that you are bothered about them and that you genuinely care about them is critical to them buying into you and the school's approach.

PS

33: REWARDS

Issuing pupils with rewards and praise can generate mixed responses and views. Some people will argue that your reward or praise should be self-generated and intrinsic. While I understand this stance, I also question it. I would pose the following question to you: if you were performing beyond the expectations of your role and no one acknowledged this at all, how would you feel? Praise and rewards should, of course, be proportionate and commensurate, and they should be sporadically applied. You should not issue praise or rewards cheaply or loosely, otherwise you will undermine their significance and worth.

SOME KEY CONSIDERATIONS

As a school you should consider carefully what you believe to be worthy of praise and/or a reward. Think carefully about your context and what would have the greatest impact on positive behaviours.	You should consider a tiered approach towards rewards, so pupils understand what they are being rewarded for and why they are being rewarded. The rewards issued should be incrementally more significant as a pupil achieves more and more.
Consider carefully the communication and training that you will employ for all stakeholders.	Do you reward pupils for academic achievement, effort, school-wide matters, community work or a cocktail of all of these behaviours?

WARNING

Children, irrespective of their age, ultimately like to be praised, like to show off positively and like rewards. Children can swiftly become disillusioned if they feel that their hard work and efforts are not acknowledged, nor rewarded. Communicating with home is a powerful approach as positive behaviours can then be rewarded at home as well.

ADVICE

Rewards do not have to carry a monetary value. It could be that you have a system in place where pupils will receive a certificate or a letter home or hot chocolate and cakes with the head. These are just a few examples. You could issue staff with three golden tickets that they can hand out in any one academic term or year to pupils for something extraordinary. You could have a star of the lesson or a star of the week and a trophy that goes home.

PS

34: THOUGHT FOR THE WEEK

Do you have a thought for the week as a school? If not, perhaps this is something you should consider. Ideally it should form a focal point, on a weekly basis, for driving an element of your school's values, culture, ethos, British values and the character of your pupils. It should serve to reinforce the behaviours you expect to see exhibited across your school community. However, if the thought for the week is something that is sent out via a weekly bulletin, read out loud and little is then done with it, it won't have any impact.

IDEAS TO EMBED YOUR THOUGHT FOR THE WEEK

Clearly map your thought for the week against your school values and ensure that you revisit each weekly thought time and again.	Theme your tutor time delivery around the thought for the week.
Theme your assemblies around the thought for the week.	Ask subject areas to map the thought for the week into their lesson delivery.

WARNING

Do not circulate a thought for the week in an ad hoc fashion. It should be part of a well-thought-out school-wide strategy, otherwise it will not succeed.

ADVICE

Take the time to train staff in how to deliver the thought for the week, be it via tutor times, assemblies or via lesson delivery. There needs to be a clarity and consistency to how this theme is narrated to the pupils.

35: ALTERNATIVE PROVISION/ALTERNATIVE SUPPORT

It is important to carefully consider what support you offer to those pupils who have complex needs, learning difficulties or those pupils who are repeat offenders. For some children continual sanctions have very limited impact in redirecting their behaviour. This is not to excuse the behaviours nor am I suggesting that you should not sanction the pupil, but it is really important to consider how you support particular pupils. You do need to consider how you make reasonable adjustments to accommodate their needs (within reason) and to consider how inclusive your overall approach is. It is therefore key that for some pupils you look carefully at how you overcome their barriers to learning.

SOME KEY CONSIDERATIONS TO SUPPORT PUPILS

Do you utilise external, Ofsted-registered, alternative provision? Given the overall cost of some alternative provision places, are you able to offer your own in-house provision?	How do you support mental health issues? Do you have counsellors on site to support children, and mental health nurses to support pupils with more complex needs? Do you have a targeted provision in place for pupils that require it?
How do you support repeat offenders with anger management: social skills, improving their behaviour or emotional coaching?	What do you do to support pupils who lack self-esteem, confidence and motivation?
How do you support pupils to learn about protective behaviours?	How do you support pupils who are underachieving due to their complex needs or wider issues?

WARNING

Do not assume that in providing wider additional support for key pupils that you are compromising your holistic standards and values as a school. If anything, you are reinforcing them with an enhanced provision offer.

ADVICE

It is really important that you do not set vulnerable and SEND children up to fail. Not all pupils can instantly cope with the demands of a full school day, and they will need the school's support.

S

36: ADDITIONAL SUPPORT

Some pupils will choose to misbehave because they cannot access the curriculum. For example, if a pupil in a maths class does not know that $6 \times 6 = 36$, then how can they access and successfully engage with fractions? If a pupil in a Year 9 history lesson has the reading age of a 7-year-old, yet the workbook or textbook they are using is written with an average reading age of 13 as the target audience, then how can they successfully read, comprehend and interpret what is in front of them? When children are presented with clear barriers that prohibit their ability to engage with the curriculum, it is often more likely than not that they will disengage from the lesson, not complete any work or misbehave. It is all too easy for a school to put the onus on the class teacher to rectify this issue through the differentiation that they employ from one lesson to the next. However, pushing class teachers to solely deal with this matter, given that they are likely to have 30 plus pupils within a class to contend with, is unlikely to yield the outcome that you want. So, what are you, the mothership, doing about it?

Key question: As the mothership, what programmes of support do you have in place to support children to catch up with their peers, specifically focusing on literacy and numeracy?

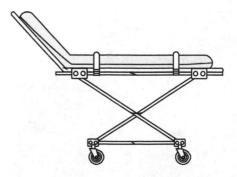

SOLUTIONS

Direct Instruction: This is a specific and targeted programme of support that can be employed in KS2/3. This programme focuses on literacy and/or numeracy. The teacher takes centre stage, with lessons deliberately scripted.	**Teaching assistants:** Some schools employ armies of teaching assistants. You could consider training them in specific and targeted literacy and numeracy programmes, such as Fast Learning, to support small numbers of pupils every 30-60 minutes.
Post-16 pupils: Sixth formers can be trained to support pupils lower down the school with literacy and numeracy. This can be a powerful approach.	**Mentoring:** It is worth considering how leaders can serve as mentors to pupils within their school to support with literacy and numeracy. If you adopt this approach then ensure leaders are trained in how to do this.

WARNING

Where pupils are behind their peers, for example where pupils are not secondary ready, then it is important not to ignore this or think that your maths and/or English departments and subject-based differentiation will resolve this matter.

ADVICE

You need to think carefully as a school about a strategic approach to supporting children who struggle to access the curriculum. If you can support these children effectively you may find that a number of behavioural issues disappear over time as pupils become more academically confident.

S

37: STUDENT SERVICES

Some schools have a student services centre. In some schools this approach works really well. In others, it serves as an excuse for pupils to abscond from lessons claiming that they do not feel well or just want to chat with someone so they can avoid class. If you decide to create a student services drop-in approach, you need to think it through really carefully and consider, as with many of the other areas I have raised in this book, what the unintended consequences could be.

POINTS TO CONSIDER

First and foremost, you need to consider why you would want this approach and whether, ultimately, it would or could become a pseudo alternate provision/haven for pupils seeking to truant their lessons.	You need to carefully consider which staff run your student services provision and which member of your senior team line-manages this provision.
It is important to consider the times of the day when student services is open to the pupils and whether there is a drop-in approach and/or a more proactive referral system.	You should keep clear logs to detect patterns and trends among groups of pupils, year groups and key pupils to see if there are genuine recurring issues and whether there are safeguarding concerns at hand.

WARNING

If you have a student services approach that is available all day long and operates in an unregulated manner, then you need to monitor carefully if pupils are using this approach as a smokescreen to avoid their lessons.

ADVICE

If you do set up or have a student services provision, you need to narrate both explicitly and clearly with pupils and staff alike what the provision is, what it offers, when it is available (think this through carefully) and who it is available to. The staff that run this service should have specialist training.

S

38: TIMETABLING

The school timetable is, especially in a large secondary school, a bit like a giant Rubik's Cube. How the timetable works for pupils and staff can have a huge impact on how pupils behave and their learning. In this section I am going to pose a number of questions and leave you some space to consider your thoughts, as follows:

- Do you have a two-week timetable? If you do, how do pupils and staff genuinely cope with a timetable that changes every other week? Can both groups remember which week it is?
- Where and how have you positioned your subjects? Is this productive and effective?
- What is the lesson allocation that you have given to your subject domains? Is this effective?
- Are staff moving around the pupils or vice versa?
- Are more inexperienced staff being given the more challenging sets and groups?
- Do you set or stream your classes?
- How many times do pupils move in the school day? Is this an effective use of time?
- Would longer lessons work in your setting? Would the time be productively used if lessons were longer?
- If you have longer lessons, does this work?
- How long do you give pupils to transition across the school, from one lesson to the next?

YOUR THOUGHTS: PLEASE USE THE FOLLOWING SPACE TO JOT DOWN SOME OF YOUR CONSIDERATIONS

_____

_____

_____

_____

_____

_____

_____

_____

_____

_____

_____

_____

_____

WARNING

Children can struggle with endless change. They feel safe and secure when there is certainty, continuity and consistency. The more change that you create due to timetabling, the more unsettled you could make your pupils.

ADVICE

Carefully consider if a two-week timetable is sensible. While you may be able to fit more in, it can be hard for staff and pupils to remember whether it is week 1 or week 2.

39: BLAMING STAFF

Staff make mistakes. All teachers make mistakes. If a pupil misbehaves in their class, you can either defend and protect a colleague or you can lay blame at their door. I worry hugely when the narrative shifts to 'Could you have made your lesson more exciting or engaging?' or 'What else could you have done to prevent that situation arising?' Or 'Do you not think you caused that situation where pupil X attacked pupil Y?' As leaders we have to be really careful with the narrative that we employ. Blaming teachers where things go wrong – and at times they will – is not helpful. Even if the teacher has caused a situation to escalate, it is better to consider how we can move forwards than it is to lay blame at the teacher's door.

IMPORTANT CONSIDERATIONS

If you consistently blame staff for issues in your school, then the leaders of the school will dampen staff morale or, at worst, lose the support of the staffing body.	Where staff are not backed up, parents will go straight to leaders over issues that they do not agree with as a means of undermining the staff.
How often do you reflect on the mistakes you may have made as a leader if staff are not implementing an approach correctly? Perhaps you need to go back to the drawing board and retrain or reboot the staffing body?	The vast majority of teachers want to do the very best job that they can and will be their own worst critics.

WARNING

You need to carefully consider the kind of culture and ethos that you want to generate in your school. A culture of blame can swiftly become toxic.

ADVICE

Where staff make mistakes, and they will, always consider carefully how you can support them. Consider what can be learned from the situation at hand and what the learning point is moving forwards.

40: PLATFORMING STAFF: THE TEACHER IS THE EXPERT

As a leader, you need to carefully consider the language that you employ to publicly platform your staff. If you refer to teachers as learning guides or facilitators, then you are downplaying their role, significance and importance. In my view, teachers should be positively hailed and platformed in front of the pupils and parents. The children need to know that they are lucky to have such a fantastic set of staff supporting their learning. They need to know that the teacher in front of them is an expert in their field, knows their stuff and is there for the children. In changing the narrative with pupils, leaders can change the mindset and therefore how pupils view the staff, both for better and worse. This can have a direct impact on behaviour.

USEFUL NARRATION

The following phrases can be really powerful in platforming staff:

- 'Your teacher is the expert in the classroom.'
- 'You should show your teacher the utmost level of respect.'
- 'Remember to always say please and thank you when addressing staff.'
- 'We are really lucky to have the staff/teachers that we do.'
- 'Your teacher has expert knowledge; you need to listen to their every word.'

WARNING

Do not undermine the role and importance of the staff in your school. Staffing accounts for 70-80% of your school budget. That is a significant level of expenditure and investment.

ADVICE

Constantly narrate to the pupils that manners maketh person. The role of manners is critical in how staff should and deserve to be addressed. Do not condone nor allow rudeness.

41: TEACHER WORKLOAD

Teacher workload is a hotly contested and debated topic among members of the profession. Workload, especially when excessive and lacking any real sense of purpose, can create huge anxiety. It can be suffocating. Leaders must create a set of working conditions and parameters that allow staff to focus on their core job, namely teaching. It is important to remember that the classroom is where the magic happens. A stark reality in our schools is if staff are swamped then they will not have the time nor the capacity to chase up pupils for behavioural matters. Leaders need to consider systems and approaches to workload and behaviour that allow staff to be freed up so they can focus on the curriculum. My own view is that you should try and keep things as simple, clear and focused as possible, with as little white noise in lessons as possible (ideally none). Staff also need to see that there are clear, easily understood and staged systems in place and that there is always lots of support and follow-through when they need your help.

SOME SOLUTIONS

Centralise your behaviour systems – do staff really need to be chasing this when the school can take responsibility and organise how behaviour is dealt with in a structured manner?	Devolve directed time/meetings to staff so they have time to focus on their core jobs. This will help them to really hone in on the curriculum, the schools' culture and the behavioural systems.
Centrally teach behaviour to the pupils through assemblies, induction programmes, boot camps and reboots. Every time you bring in a new expectation, centrally teach it so staff can see what the expectation is, have it modelled to them and the pupils will then have had exposure to what is expected of them. This means staff are not trying to approach things with the pupils from scratch.	Think carefully about creating a workload charter as a commitment pledge to your staff to support them and their workload. But ensure that this is a living and breathing set of approaches and not just a nice-looking document.

WARNING

Do not ignore workload or take the view that teaching should hurt. If staff do not feel supported to perform their role effectively, then you will ultimately have a morale issue on your hands and potentially a recruitment and retention issue.

ADVICE

Think about Maslow's hierarchy of needs. Staff want to feel safe and work in a professional environment that allows them to reach the dizzy heights of self-actualisation.

PS

42: MARKING

Marking pupils' work can have an impact on pupil behaviour. Pupils ultimately like to receive feedback, especially on their work. When pupils do not receive regular and timely feedback, it can lead to disgruntlement, a lack of engagement and a sense that the teacher does not really care. This can impact on the relationships that are at play between a teacher and the pupils. It is therefore important to carefully consider the marking and feedback policy and approach that you adopt as a school. If you have an approach that is labour intensive, you are potentially throwing your staff under the bus and setting an unrealistic expectation that the pupils themselves will cite back to the staff as a means of holding them to account. This can be dangerous and cause you and your staff many issues.

SOLUTIONS AND CONSIDERATIONS

Whole-class feedback: This approach can seriously reduce the volume of marking and the time teachers have to spend on marking.	**Live feedback in lessons:** There is extensive research that shows this is a highly powerful and time-rich approach.
Removing DIRT marking as an institutional approach: This approach can carry some benefits if executed carefully but it is hugely time consuming.	Setting a realistic, not idealistic, set of parameters in place for marking cycles.

WARNING

Marking is a hugely time intensive and, at worst, time-poor approach that can have minimal impact. We need to consider the narrative and the expectations that are relayed to pupils, parents and staff regarding marking.

ADVICE

Always consider carefully what you want to prioritise as a school. If you are prioritising marking and teachers are marking every single word in a red pen or using DIRT marking all the time, then what will you remove from their plate to allow this?

PS

43: STAFF TRAINING: PART 1

You cannot assume that by simply telling staff something once, that they will understand what you want and easily drive it complication free. Realistically you need to train staff in precisely what you want and how you want it. You need to model any expectations that you wish to see displayed. Staff then need to practise, practise and practise this some more until what you want is embedded and becomes habitual.

The following diagram is a useful way of considering and remembering how to implement and embed any change you wish to see:

WARNING

If the initiative or change you are training your staff in is 'for Ofsted' or you are doing it because every other school is doing it, then your motivation and thinking could be fiercely questioned. You really need to pause, think and consider again what the motivation is and if this is truly going to bring about positive change for all. Always consider how any given change links back to your school values, vision and ethos.

ADVICE

Staff need time to consider any changes that you are seeking to bring in. They also need training. They will need to consider, as Simon Sinek[6] says, 'the why' underpinning what you are trying to achieve. This is why your mission statement, vision statement and core values are so important and integral to the changes that you are looking to bring. If you cannot justify a change as having a positive impact on the school's culture, on the pupils' learning and on the staff, then you need to seriously consider why you are bringing that change about.

44: STAFF TRAINING: PART 2

Investing in the professional development of your staff is vital. As a leader, it is always worth remembering that somewhere between 70% and 80% of your school's capitation goes on staffing. If you are not investing in and developing your staff, then you run the risk of wasting a significant chunk of your school's budget as people are being left to find things out for themselves. At the very worst, staff will have little awareness of your school's expectations, values and norms. Practice and approaches will be hugely inconsistent and varied, leading to pupils not really knowing what the expectations of them are. Equally, if you are not training your staff and investing in their professional development, how can you be sure, as a leader, that staff know and are clear on what you want, how you want it and why you want it? How do you know that your staff are clear on what your change looks like and how it will be both presented and delivered to the pupils?

OPPORTUNITIES TO TRAIN STAFF

New staff induction: Do you train all of your new staff, via an induction process, in safeguarding, behaviour, pastoral care, how to be a tutor and an outline what your school's culture is?	**INSET days:** These are an obvious opportunity for school leaders, but do you utilise these days to train staff accordingly?
Twilight training: Have you considered creating a model of twilight training that allows you to train staff in behaviour, safeguarding and student care at a level that is appropriate to them and their professional career stage, position and needs?	**Briefings:** Are all of your briefings simply conveying messages or do you use this time to deliver short, sharp training sessions for your staff?
Staff meetings: Do you use this time purposefully and effectively to train staff in your systems, culture, climate and ethos?	**Reboots:** Do you purposefully look to reboot the culture of your school and, in turn, revisit key aspects of training with staff?

WARNING

Do not assume staff can and will know how your school, its systems and processes work. Assumption is the mother of all stuff-ups. As a leader, it is important to remember that you are in a position to offer your staff high levels of support.

ADVICE

Consider carefully the external training you will send your staff on and the external speakers you may decide to utilise and bring into your school to support your cultural drive. You should also carefully consider the specific and bespoke training needs of your staff.

45: OPEN-DOOR APPROACH

How open is your school? Do teachers close their classroom door when they teach their lessons with their classroom becoming almost a vacuum? I would promote all schools to adopt an open-door policy. In other words, when teachers are teaching their classroom doors should be open. Why? Because we should operate as one school, one community and one team. Leaders should be visible and present every lesson and freely walking in and out of classrooms to ensure that staff are not struggling. Opening our doors during lesson time conveys an openness to one another. It is easy to see where another member of staff may need support. Equally, it conveys to the pupils that at any moment a senior or pastoral leader could walk into their class. Pupils will also be aware of the noise level in their lesson if the classroom door is open and this can have an impact on another class. This can help to regulate the level of unhelpful noise that emanates across the school.

Having an open-door approach should be supportive and reassuring for staff as their colleagues can hear if there is an issue and come to their aid. It should, if done right, generate a sense of collective security.

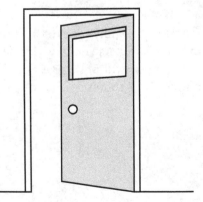

WARNING

An open-door approach will not succeed if leaders are using this as a means to identify poor practice and to vilify staff.

ADVICE

Senior leaders should lead by example here, with their door open for staff to freely come and visit their lessons. Taken a step further, senior leaders should share their timetable with the main staffing body and openly invite colleagues to watch them teach. This can generate a really positive culture and environment within a school if this is done well.

PS

46: BEING THE ADULT: BUILDING RELATIONSHIPS

Children ultimately need certainty, boundaries, consistency and for adults to behave as adults. The staff that work within a school, especially teachers, are held to a set of professional standards. The professional boundaries that we lay down with our pupils are key. If we present children with blurred lines then the behaviours we will receive and elicit from our pupils will invariably be confused.

KEY POINTS

All staff should seek to develop strong professional relationships with the children they serve. Relationships are the foundation for everything.	All staff should adhere to their school's code of conduct, which should include professional attire.
Staff should act as role models for the pupils and embody the values, vision and ethos of the school.	Staff should always, as part of their safeguarding duty, keep the children that make up the school community safe.

WARNING

When staff try to portray themselves as a friend or one of the gang with pupils, they undermine their position and ultimately the level of respect that the pupils will show them. It is key that leaders are clear on the expectations on and of their staffing body, provide training on this and follow through on issues.

ADVICE

It is important that leaders instil in their staffing bodies the highest levels of professionalism and professional standards. The starting point should always be the formulation of professional working relationships. Without relationships in place, it is very challenging to generate buy-in.

PS

47: UNIFORM: YES OR NO?

School uniform can bring about many heated debates. Critics of school uniforms cite the unaffordable cost of decking a child out for school and question what educational benefit it yields. However, a big issue among children, especially teenagers, is that they are conformist. The price of the latest Nike trainers alone can be more than a full school uniform. I would argue that uniform brings about a sense of community, cohesion and identity and, importantly, it is a social leveller within a school setting. Of course children can work out who lives in the biggest house etc., but within the context of a school day, if they are all wearing the same uniform, then these socio-economic divides are not as stark and obvious.

Uniform also helps bring about a common sense of identity that we all belong to school X. If our narration of our school's values is strong and consistent, then this can breed a sense of pride, which can permeate beyond the school gates and into the wider community.

CONSIDERATIONS AND THOUGHTS

Uniform should be affordable for families.	Consider a uniform that is comfortable. If children are fidgeting all day due to a scratchy and uncomfortable uniform, then they will be distracted.
In a larger school you could add a year group badge or flash to the uniform so it is obvious which year group pupils belong to. This can greatly assist staff in managing behaviour.	Ensure your uniform approach is carefully communicated to families and done so in a timely manner. Also, keep your uniform approach consistent so parents are not having to continually chop and change and so they can pass uniform to younger siblings.

WARNING

It is important to carefully consider where the cost of uniform could serve as a barrier to pupils accessing education and ensure that you have an approach as a school to support with this.

ADVICE

It is important to carefully consider the purpose that your uniform serves and why you insist on one. As pupils progress through the school, you may wish to adapt the uniform to signify who the oldest year group are, for example a different coloured shirt. Pupils, in my experience, like this and see it as a rite of passage.

S

48: EQUIPPING PUPILS

A number of schools have a 'ready to learn' or 'be prepared' style motto. I understand fully the necessity of being ready for school and taking pride in your learning. However, it is important to consider carefully how you ensure that the most disadvantaged pupils are supported to be 'ready to learn'. How you help and support your Pupil Premium pupils here is key. Pupil Premium funding is issued to schools to remove barriers to learning. Being 'ready to learn' can present a huge barrier for your pupils if they do not even have enough food to eat at home.

SOME CONSIDERATIONS

Can you equip every pupil with a clear pencil case? They will need one for their public exams.	Can you equip pupils with the pens, pencils and other relevant stationery that they need?
Can you equip pupils with a book bag to carry all of their school-based items in? This then means all pupils would have the same bag as opposed to some having the latest £70 Nike backpack and some not even having a bag at all.	It is worthwhile speaking to subject teachers across the curriculum to ascertain what stationery demands are actually placed on pupils so that they are 'ready to learn'.

WARNING

If, as a school, you are not prepared to support pupils with essential stationery, then how will you respond to pupils who are not appropriately equipped for school? You could find that you are sanctioning (if that is your course of action) a number of pupils who otherwise would not be sanctioned if you were to provide this essential equipment as a school.

ADVICE

You would be surprised by the number of companies that are prepared to issue schools with stationery, either at a reduced cost or for free. As a leader, do your homework here.

PS

49: USING YOUR SCHOOL BUILDING TO SUPPORT BEHAVIOUR

Is a school building just a building, just a set of rooms, just a myriad of corridors? A school building can so easily be overlooked as part of your overall approach to behaviour and how it can be utilised to good effect to support behaviour. In this section I am going to pose a number of questions and give you my views regarding how you can use a building to support you, as follows:

- Where do you base your teachers? My own view is that year groups (in a primary phase) or subject teams should be placed in the same area of the school. On one front this helps to create a sense of identity. In equal measure it means that members of staff are not having to roam the school from lesson to lesson. I have been a classroom nomad before and every lesson I lost 10 minutes of learning time, through no fault of my own, ferrying across the school site and setting up my lesson in front of my class.

- Where do you base your tutors? I would argue that year groups should ideally belong to one subject group and that this subject team should oversee the year group from their entry to the school until they finish the school. This allows you to build and create a sense of identity among a year group, and it supports leaders to know where a year group is based during tutor time. It also means that the pupils have a degree of consistency and continuity, with the same tutor overseeing them from the start of their school experience until they leave the school. This is a powerful approach for any school to take.

- How many display boards do you have? I would personally argue, at a secondary level at least, keeping display boards to a minimum. You need to carefully consider the cognitive overload on pupils and, simultaneously, the workload factor for staff. You should also consider carefully what you actually display. My own view is that the school's mission statement, values and class expectations/rules should be on display in every single room and that there may be a tutor group notice board and a board displaying pupil work. I am not sure the average classroom needs much more than this.

- Do you employ the use of a one-way system? Certainly in larger schools I do believe that this serves a purpose and prevents an excessive contraflow of pupils making a corridor unsafe.

- How regularly do you have the school cleaned? I would argue (and I appreciate that there is a cost attached here) to have the school regularly cleaned throughout the school day. This signifies to the pupils that you value the school and so should they.

- Do you have open-plan toilets? This is very context specific and a lot can depend on the culture of the school when considering this approach.

- Where do you position pastoral and senior leader offices? This requires a lot of thought and you want them to be close to the areas that they oversee/line manage.

WARNING

Failing to consider how your building works to your advantage will ultimately undermine you.

ADVICE

Consider carefully your entry and exit points for the start and end of the school day. The manner in which pupils enter and leave the school will have an impact on your school's culture.

PS

50: UNSTRUCTURED TIME: LUNCH

Unstructured points in the school day can present a real headache for school leaders. At times it can feel almost contradictory that you have tight systems and structures in place during lesson time, but as soon as lunch arrives an entire school community is allowed to mix without any real sense of structure, routine or system. There are many key considerations to ponder on when considering how lunch at your school can work, as follows:

- How long should the lunch break be? An hour? 40 minutes? 30 minutes? It is worth considering the length of your lunch break and where/when issues present themselves or if it is too short.

- Where do pupils consume their food? Do you have different zones within your school where pupils can eat a packed lunch, a hot dinner or a sandwich-style meal deal?

- Who is on duty? How many senior leaders and pastoral staff are present during a lunchtime sitting? What role do other staff play in supporting the duty rota?

- You must carefully consider contractual obligations too. If staff are, for example, on standard teacher terms and conditions, then they should not conduct a duty post 12.00pm.

- Do you allow one or two year groups or classes out at a time? Do you have split or rotating lunches?

- Do you want pupils to be sat while they eat?

- Do you adopt a 'family dining' style approach or do you see this as too prohibitive?

- Do you want a longer lunch so staff can offer clubs and activities? If this is the case, what does this say about your approach to workload?

- Do you finish a lunch period off with a line-up to recalibrate a group of pupils before they go back into their lessons?

WARNING

If you know that there are issues within your school during unstructured times and you do not look to rectify these, then you are essentially stating, whether you like to admit this or not, that lunch is not a priority.

ADVICE

It is important to carefully consider the space and facilities that you have at your disposal when considering your holistic approach to how lunches operate.

51: TUTOR PERIODS/THE ROLE OF THE TUTOR

Many schools have a tutor time slot in their school day. Many schools cite just how important and relevant their tutors are. I would subscribe firmly to the view and stance that tutors play a vital role in the delivery of the school's wider curriculum and help to reinforce the school's culture, ethos, vision and values. For any given school you can adopt a number of stances for your tutors and tutor periods, as follows:

1. Tutor time can be used as an extended session of pastoral care, where tutors build relationships with their tutees and deal with pastoral matters. They are also a chance for pupils to speak with one another.

2. Tutor time is a structured part of the school day, with tutors expected to plan a tutor time session on a daily basis to deliver to their pupils.

3. Tutor time is a structured part of the school day, with tutor sessions centrally planned, following a clear and consistent programme of study from one year group to the next.

4. A hybrid of the above.

My own view is that tutor time should be centrally planned. If your student care and pastoral systems are suitably strong enough across your school, then there should be less of a need – though perhaps not no need – for tutor time to serve as a pastoral-based session.

WARNING

Tutor time can account for almost 15 to 20 minutes a day. If you leave this time to chance and do not have this part of your day centrally planned, how can you be confident that this is an effective and beneficial use of time?

ADVICE

If you want your tutor time delivery to be high quality, purposeful, consistent and to carry real meaning, then centrally plan it so every tutor group in any one given year group is doing the same thing on any one given day. Have a clear plan for every week and a clear plan for every term. Also, ensure that tutors are provided with quality, regular and timely training so they can perform their role effectively.

S

52: ASSEMBLIES

Assemblies are a hugely powerful tool and should take place as regularly and frequently as possible. They support the overall community feel of a school and bring about a sense of identity and belonging. They can take many shapes and forms, be they for a year group, a key stage, a vertical house or for specific groups of pupils. While it is hugely important for senior leaders to be present and to deliver assemblies, I would also argue that other members of staff, be they middle leaders or teaching staff, should have the opportunity to deliver them. While delivering assemblies is an art form, the opportunity to deliver them serves as another invaluable form of professional development for colleagues. Assemblies play an integral part in securing, driving and embedding a school's culture, expectations and norms. They also represent an opportunity to champion the children in your school and their successes. Assemblies provide schools with a real opportunity to explore issues and topics in more detail and to further enrich the curriculum. They also provide teachers with the opportunity to train pupils in expected school-based norms.

KEY ASSEMBLY FUNCTIONS

Assemblies offer schools the opportunity to present and train pupils in new systems, expectations, values and norms.	Assemblies can, and should, be used to narrate expectations, to remind pupils of school rules and routines, and can be used to train children in your systems.
Assemblies should reinforce the school's values and ethos. While they should arguably hang on a fundamental theme, they should serve to reinforce what your school is about and generate a community identity.	Assemblies should educate the pupils in an area of character development that will ultimately enhance their learning and develop them into more rounded and better-behaved members of the school community.

WARNING

Do not see assemblies as a waste of 15 minutes, where solely messages (bulletin style) are to be relayed to children. They are a hugely valuable part of the school day and often afford you the opportunity to recalibrate the school community.

ADVICE

When delivering an assembly, keep in mind that the assembly is as much for the staff as it is for the pupils. They offer you an opportunity to narrate key messages that both stakeholders need to know, understand and remember.

S

53: LINE-UPS

Some schools nationally employ the use of line-ups. They tend to be used at the start of the school day, after any given break period and/or lunch. Some schools will use line-ups with their entire school community, other schools use them with particular year groups or particular key stages. Normally they are conducted outside, in an open-space area. Naturally, therefore, the one cautionary point regarding line-ups is that they are normally suspended if there is inclement weather. The aim and purpose of a line-up is, to my mind, fivefold:

- To bring about calm, order and routine at the start of the day and/ or following a break.
- To allow swift movement and transitions into the school building.
- To afford leaders the opportunity to deliver short, sharp, snappy messages in real-time to staff and pupils alike.
- To recalibrate pupils so that they are ready to learn.
- To allow staff to check pupil uniform and equipment.

WHAT ARE LINE-UPS?

Line-ups are where pupils stand in single-file lines either as a tutor group or a class set.	Form tutors or class teachers should stand at the front of each line so pupils know where to stand.
A senior leader should stand on a bench and blow a whistle for the pupils to fall silent. The senior leader should then deliver a clear two-minute message linked to the school's values or cover a real-time matter that needs addressing.	Staff should check pupil attire and equipment. The senior leader in charge of the line-up should then dismiss the tutor groups/classes one group at a time to enter the school building.

WARNING

Do not assume that pupils and staff will know how to conduct a line-up without suitable training in how to do so.

ADVICE

Leaders should consider in advance key institutional messages that they wish to convey to the pupils. Line-ups offer an invaluable opportunity for daily messaging and your sound bites should reinforce the school's ethos.

PS

54: WHERE TO DRAW THE LINE?

A big challenge for schools is defining where their remit begins and ends. It is important to consider whether issues that occur outside the school grounds after the school day has ended are the school's responsibility to resolve or whether they should fall into the laps of parents. I do think for any given school this is hugely challenging and can bring about multiple moral dilemmas for any leadership team. What happens beyond the school gates often has a real bearing and impact on the school day. So many external issues can very easily end up spilling into the running of the school, and very often members of the community will look to the school to resolve issues, take responsibility and reprimand poor behaviour.

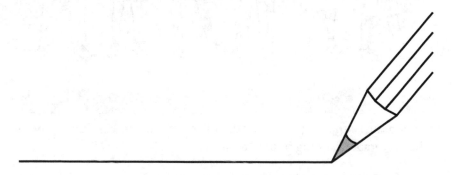

KEY CONSIDERATIONS

It is important to discuss and debate as a leadership team where your remit begins and ends, and to discuss this with trust boards.	You should take the time to relate to the pupils their responsibilities and explain that when they are in the community they represent the school, especially if they are wearing the school's uniform.
It is worth considering forging links with the local police force. Some schools have successfully created Safer School Partnership networks and appointed their own PCSOs.	Consider carefully how you police your school site at the start and end of the school day. Also contemplate how far away from the school grounds you want duty staff to be.

WARNING

If you do take the view that issues outside school hours have nothing to do with the school, then carefully consider what message this sends to pupils and what the unintended consequences of this may be.

ADVICE

My own personal view is that I would take the time to deal with issues outside the parameters of the school day and, where applicable, involve the police. In ignoring matters you are potentially creating and allowing bigger issues to surface. It is always best to nip problems swiftly in the bud.

PS

55: TRANSITION

We tend to think of transition at key crunch points, for example, starting in EYFS, starting in Year 7 or starting in Year 12. These are obvious transition points in any given child's educational career. However, we can be guilty of forgetting what it is like to transition from one academic year to the next and from one key stage to the next. In this section I want to pose some important considerations for you as a leader. It is not really possible to give all of the answers as every context is different, but sparking your thinking here is important.

CONSIDERATIONS

- How do you induct new pupils into your school, not just at crunch points such as the start of Year 7, but also when a new pupil joins mid-year?
- What does your induction programme look like and consist of, and how long does it last?
- Does your induction programme contain behavioural training sessions? Sessions on values, norms, expectations? If so, how do you narrate these to the pupils and how much of your established norms do you physically train your new cohort of pupils in to ensure that they know your standards and expectations?
- Do you provide parents with information at transition points? Do you deliver talks to them outlining your school's expectations? Do key staff front-load their communication with home to strike a rapport?

- How do you support pupils as they transition through your school and from one key stage to the next? How do you front-load this?
- Do you see transition as a one-hit wonder or part of a longer-term process, which you constantly revisit?
- Have you planned in reboots for pupils at strategic points in the year to revisit your expectations, values and norms?
- Do you, following a break, stagger the reintroduction of pupils so you can recalibrate the behaviours that you want to see exhibited in your school?
- Who actually leads the training and talks that you deliver? Is the head involved? Are senior leaders involved?

WARNING

If you do not carefully and meticulously plan transition across your school, then you cannot expect pupils to know what you want nor what it looks like. You run the risk of leaving it to chance or devolving this to staff who may not consistently deliver your main messages, especially if you have not taken the time to train them.

ADVICE

Create a clear template and plan for how you want transition to look, when it needs to take place and what you want to achieve from your transition arrangements. Also, do not be frightened, following a lengthy holiday, to slow the taught curriculum down and deliver reboots to the children.

PS

56: OFSTED QUESTIONS

In this section, I wanted to share with you some of the questions Ofsted could ask you during an inspection or, indeed, that could be posed to you by an external school improvement adviser. It is important to note that every school and every inspection team is different, so this is not an exact science.

POSSIBLE QUESTIONS

- How does your behaviour system work? Talk me through how it is tiered, staggered and managed.
- Does your behaviour system work? How do you know?
- Is behaviour management consistent across your school? How do you know?
- What training and support do you give to your staff? How effective is this? What impact has it had?
- Do you utilise any external support? If so, who? What has their impact been?
- Have you conducted any external reviews of behaviour? What are the trends?
- What are the trends and themes coming from your exclusion/sanction/attendance data?
- When issues arise with behaviour, how do you respond as a school?
- How do you support pupils?
- How do you support children with special educational needs?

- How do you support vulnerable pupils and disadvantaged pupils?
- How do you support pupils to tackle bullying, harassment and homophobia?
- How is behaviour improving? Can you evidence this?
- Can you provide case studies for pupils who have been suspended?
- How is your behaviour policy adapted by age and stage, if applicable?
- Show me your EHE (electively home educated) logs.

WARNING

Please do not do things in your school because you think it will please Ofsted or because that is what Ofsted wants. Invariably the 'this is what Ofsted wants' line creates a false narrative, with senior leaders acquiring third-hand knowledge that does not reflect what Ofsted will actually look for.

ADVICE

I personally believe that it is important to hold firm and true to your values and beliefs. If you have a high suspension rate, for example, this does not necessarily mean that your school is in a crisis. There may be perfectly justifiable reasons for a high exclusion/suspension rate that are firmly linked to your values and expectations as a school. Ensure that you clearly narrate these.

PS

57: QUALITY ASSURANCE

Leaders have to quality assure their schools to know that things are working and have to be able to evidence that approaches are effective, that the curriculum is being delivered successfully and that behaviour, critically, is positive. This does not mean that leaders have to walk in and out of classrooms with a clipboard, engaging in high-stake judgements and create a climate where people feel that they are being watched continuously with conclusions created about their performance management. The following offers you some ideas of how you can quality assure your school's behaviour.

QUALITY ASSURANCE SOLUTIONS

Being positively visible: If you are regularly walking the school, visiting lessons, on duty, in lessons etc., then you can very quickly piece together a holistic feel for where behaviour is at.	**Surveys:** There are pros and cons to issuing any survey but they can provide you with valuable and confidential information that can help to inform your next steps.
Talk: Do not underestimate the power of talking (provided people trust you). If you have generated a positive culture in your school then staff and pupils will be open and honest with you about behaviour and what it is like.	**External support:** Ask another leader from another school to come in and dip sample the climate of your school. Invite trustees into the school to do this too. Speak to supply teachers to see how they are treated by the pupils.

WARNING

If you have identified an issue do not ignore it. For example, if your quality assurance identifies a lack of awareness about e-safety or a need to develop a package of Protective Behaviour support, then it would be remiss not to action this.

ADVICE

Take the time to look carefully at your in-house behavioural tracking data to detect trends, themes and patterns.

PS

58: ATTENDANCE

Attendance is hugely important. There is ultimately no adequate substitute for face-to-face learning in a classroom setting and the more time children are off from school, the further behind they will fall with their learning. If you were to forensically examine your attendance data against exam outcomes for the pupils who attend your school, I am certain that you would see a direct correlation between high levels of attendance and positive exam outcomes. In my experience, the GCSE outcomes of Year 11 pupils are strongest where their attendance is 96% or more. Attendance data can also be used to detect patterns, trends and potential safeguarding issues. For some pupils, being in school is the safest place for them given their home setting (or lack of one). It is therefore critically important that schools have clear and robust attendance procedures and systems in place.

KEY CONSIDERATIONS

Do you have a clearly tiered attendance system in place, where key members of staff action attendance concerns at set thresholds?	Do you have a first day response approach and do you have staff, for example educational welfare officers, who will undertake home visits and welfare checks for pupils who are absent?
Do you have senior leader involvement in your attendance processes and routines?	Do you externally audit your attendance protocols and procedures to ensure that your practice is sharp?

WARNING

If you ignore attendance issues when they are in their infancy, the chances are they will snowball and escalate into a much bigger and deeper issue that will ultimately take you even longer to rectify and resolve.

ADVICE

If your local authority offers little real support then it may pay you to consider looking at employing the services of a legal team.

S

59: REPORT SYSTEMS

A number of schools utilise reports as a means of monitoring, redirecting and correcting pupil behaviour. Reports can be a powerful tool to help keep a watchful eye on a pupil, as well as a means of detecting if there are patterns or continual issues in certain subject areas or at certain points in a day or a week. They can also help leaders to gather information and evidence that can be utilised to support interventions and/or sanctions. This evidence can also help form part of the narrative that you will engage parents/families in. It is important that you tier your reporting system and have pupils on report for set periods of time, for example, 10 school days. The idea of having a tiered system is to support colleagues should they hit a glass ceiling with a pupil and to signify to a pupil the ever-increasing seriousness of the escalation process.

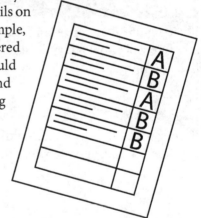

EXAMPLE REPORT STAGES

The following serves as a guide to demonstrate how you could tier your reporting cycle, with a pupil on report for 10 days at each stage:

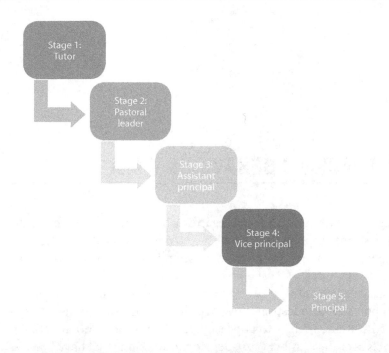

It is really important that you spell out to a pupil what they are on report for and to issue them with key targets to focus on while they are on report. Whenever a pupil goes on report, irrespective of the stage that they are on, communication should be made with home.

Always ensure that all staff know that a pupil is on report and why they are on report. Placing pupils on report can also be an effective mechanism for those pupils who fly below the radar behaviour-wise. For example, you may have a system as a school where you warn and then sanction. What happens to those pupils who receive a warning every single day to monitor and positively redirect their behaviour?

PS

60: TRACKING BEHAVIOUR DATA

Tracking information and data regarding behaviour can serve as a double-edged sword. Schools should be wary of tracking data as a means of bringing, for example, suspension or detention data sets down just because a table says a lot of suspensions or detentions have occurred. When schools seek to reduce the number of suspensions or detentions issued, then one should question why. Are they doing this because they think Ofsted will like it? Is it to appease a local authority who are challenging schools over the number of suspensions/exclusions that have been issued? Is there an attempt to create a false sense that behaviour is better than it is? What behaviours are being ignored and what impact is this having on teachers, pupils and lesson delivery? Data should inform where there are behavioural issues in a school and where support, input and training are required. It should also be used to proactively pre-empt issues. For example, if you know that Year 9 on a Friday period 5 are an issue for a particular subject area/teacher, then what will you proactively do, using this localised knowledge, to intervene and support?

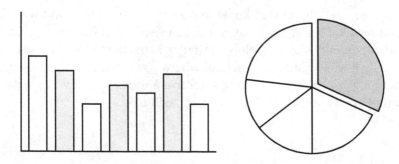

HOW CAN BEHAVIOUR DATA BE USED EFFECTIVELY?

Data can be used to inform programmes of support for pupils with behavioural difficulties.	Data can be utilised to show you which staff are actually sticking to the school's behaviour policy and potentially where staff are not using it.
If there are repeated or common incidences within a school you can use this data to inform your curriculum design and delivery to address these issues.	Data can help to inform seasonal trends and issues.

WARNING

Try to avoid immediately assuming that a high number of punitive sanctions means a school is in crisis or a subject area is weak. This could be a sign that a school or a subject team have incredibly high standards and are extremely consistent in their approach.

ADVICE

Data trends can be really useful to pre-empt seasonal issues that arise year in, year out. This information can help to inform staff training, programmes of support and assembly themes. In my experience November and January tend to be the most challenging months of the year for pupil behaviour.

PS

61: BEHAVIOURAL RESEARCH GROUP

Research is really important. Considering both research and evidence can support your overall holistic approach to behaviour. It can also help to save you a lot of time through avoiding a process of trial and error. A key question to ponder on is how seriously do you really take behaviour and research? If you truly value your research then perhaps you should put your money where your mouth is, metaphorically speaking. You could invest in a group of staff by creating a research group who are tasked with looking into the most up-to-date and relevant research in and around behaviour who could do a lot of the leg work for you. How many schools are willing to create a research team and give them the time, freedom and space to thoroughly consider the research in and around behaviour (or any other area) and test it out to see what does or does not work within their context?

IDEAS FOR SETTING UP A RESEARCH GROUP

Identify one member of staff to head up an internally based research group.	Consider carefully how you will allow them to function. For example, what time, funding, CPD opportunities and space will you allow them?
Consider carefully how you market the research group to your staff to attract broader interest across the full bandwidth of your staffing body.	Staff should be given the intellectual freedom and space to explore an area of behaviour and the underpinning research of their choosing. Otherwise they will not own this.

WARNING

Do not dictate to staff what their lines of enquiry will be, otherwise this research group will become your research group and not the staffing body's.

ADVICE

Invite staff to visit other schools. Do take an active interest in their work and findings. Importantly, consider how you can platform their work to inform the school's strategic direction and train the staff as a whole.

PS

62: BEHAVIOUR CHARTER

A behaviour charter is in essence a one-side chart detailing your approach to behaviour, student care and safeguarding. It is a commitment pledge to your staff, parents and pupils and an ideal that you will not only strive to work towards to but, importantly, uphold and use as a benchmark to judge yourself, the school and your provision against.

KEY IDEAS FOR A BEHAVIOUR CHARTER

- You should create an almost grid-like charter that has four or five pillars.
- You should consider carefully what your pillars are, but broadly speaking I would encourage you to have the following: safety and wellbeing, behaviour, curriculum/wider curriculum, training and pastoral care.
- Each pillar should detail, in bullet-point fashion, the main elements of your provision and offers as a school.
- Your charter should also outline key elements of research that have underpinned your thinking.

WARNING

Do not produce your charter in isolation. This will cease to mean anything to the staff if this is written by two to three members of staff only.

ADVICE

Allow staff to input their ideas and advice so they own the document as much as the leadership team do. Come back to this charter on a regular basis to keep it fresh, up to date and reflective of the staff who are working in your school.

THE MOTHERSHIP: CONCLUDING THOUGHTS

'Leaders allow others to succeed.'

Your role as a leader is critical to the success of your institution. The behaviours that manifest themselves in your school will serve as a reflection of the culture, climate and ethos that you have generated. I am not saying that blame lies at your door when a child misbehaves, but the way that you respond to any given situation will define how you as a leader are viewed by all other respective stakeholders. I also appreciate, especially if you join a school in challenging circumstances, that the situation in front of you can seem daunting to say the least. Keep in mind that Rome was not built in a day and that slow change often leads to lasting change. There are, of course, quick wins to be had. One question you should always consider is 'Why?' You have to know why you are doing what you are doing. You must be able to narrate it with confidence and conviction. You must be able ultimately to justify it. If you cannot explain the 'why', then you need to rethink your approach. As I bring this section of the book to a close, I want to emphasise some key takeaways and common misconceptions.

KEY TAKEAWAY POINTS

1. The headteacher has to lead from the front and set the culture of the school. This then becomes a shared set of beliefs and habits as part of a lived reality shared by all. They are like the coxswain of a rowing team.

2. You must have explicitly clear and well-communicated expectations, rules and systems in place. You should provide lots of support to staff, parents and pupils alike.

3. Both staff and pupils need, and deserve, to receive lots of training in behaviour and your cultural norms.

4. Every decision you make should link explicitly and directly to your school's mission statement, vision and values. There should be a shared, collective vision.

5. It is critical that you explicitly model all of the behaviours that you expect to see so staff and pupils alike know precisely what you want.

COMMON MISCONCEPTIONS

1. Behaviour is not the responsibility of leaders *or* it is solely the responsibility of one labelled leader who drives behaviour.

2. The culture of the school is not set by the head.

3. Clear systems, rules and routines inhibit teacher creativity and are stifling.

4. All negative behaviours are either the teacher's fault for not planning their lesson effectively or a manifestation of an unmet need.

5. Expecting good standards of behaviour is oppressive.

The following details the common features shared by some of the most successful schools:

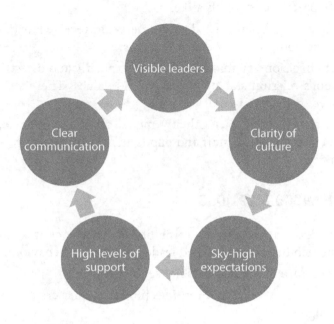

REFLECTIONS

Please use the following space, having read the mothership section, to write any key reflections or take-home points that you are considering or may action.

_____

_____

_____

_____

_____

_____

_____

_____

_____

_____

_____

_____

_____

_____

_____

_____

SECTION 2: SATELLITES
THE ROLE MIDDLE LEADERS PLAY

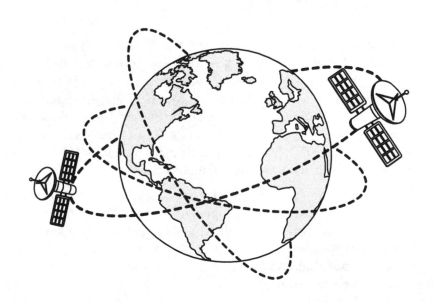

INTRODUCTION

'A leader takes people where they want to go. A great leader takes people where they don't necessarily want to go, but ought to be.'
Rosalynn Carter, Former First Lady of the USA[7]

The role middle leaders play is instrumental in school. They are often referred to as the engine room or heartbeat of a school. Middle leaders, by and large, tend to head up a house, a year group, a subject or faculty, or serve as the leader of a phase. Their role is to lead, manage, support, train and inspire the staff that work both for and with them. In equal measure, they have to answer more directly to senior leaders than class teachers potentially do. There is, in effect, no hiding place for a middle leader and their role is almost a thankless and relentless one.

Middle leaders should, ideally, have a sound command of their curriculum and sound classroom management skills. Without these two professional bedrocks, they will struggle to spin the multiple plates that they are expected to keep abreast of and will fail not only to support their team of staff, but also to model effectively to them the necessary behaviours to be successful. The role of a middle leader requires strong and constantly sound communication skills. It also requires the middle leader in charge to be able to collaborate with meaning and bring their team with them. Middle leaders must be equipped to coach, mentor and develop their teams. They also, very much as a senior leader would, need to know themselves well, including their own strengths and areas for improvement, just as much as they would their own team's strengths and areas for improvement. They should also possess – which some contest as a concept – emotional intelligence, empathy and compassion. This list of attributes can, if a middle leader operates as an island, come across as daunting and overwhelming. However, so many people make the role look effortless and seamless.

Middle leaders should be advocates of the curriculum, especially if they head up their own subject discipline. They should know the culture that they want to generate for their satellite area of the school and understand how this fits effortlessly into the wider school vision, values, ethos and mission statement. They should also promote high levels of consistency among the team that they oversee. As Robert Rosenthal[8] said there should be 'pygmalion in the classroom'. In other words, high expectations, and consistently high ones at that, have a strong impact on pupil performance.

At the heart of all that a middle leader does, they should never lose sight of what it is to be a teacher, nor should they lose sight of why they became a teacher and their overall moral purpose. These touchstones serve any middle leader well. It is important that middle leaders champion children and champion their staff. It is critical that they help to foster a learning environment that, as I have cited before in this book, allows teachers to teach, pupils to learn and the magic to happen. Without this, school improvement will fail, teachers will fail and children will fail. The responsibility and privileged position afforded to a middle leader is huge. Hence why I promote all middle leaders to read this entire book from cover to cover as you not only need to understand your role as the leader of a satellite, but also where you fit as a leader, and to always remember how class teachers have to operate on a daily basis.

In many regards, the sphere of middle leader looks as follows:

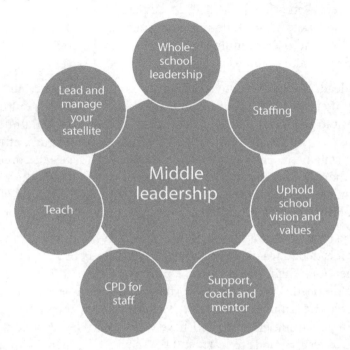

Within the multitude of hats that a middle leader has to adorn, they also have to take a direct lead on behaviour. They either have to head up a group of pupils directly, coupled with a team of staff who often serve as tutors, or they have to lead on the consistency of classroom delivery among a team of staff. In either case, middle leaders have to ensure that classroom behaviour is sound and effective, that staff have the confidence, skill set and repertoire of classroom management strategies to succeed and that pupils know precisely what is expected of them. This section of the book is designed to support middle leaders with this integral role.

PS

63: NEW TO MIDDLE LEADERSHIP

Commencing as a new middle leader can be both exciting and daunting. You have stepped up and out of being a full-time class teacher but still retain a significant teaching load. You will also have a satellite to lead and manage. You have a team of staff that you are responsible for and pupils that you need to lead and inspire, potentially as a year group or house team. As you assume your new post you may wish to consider how you establish yourself. The following flow diagram may support you with this:

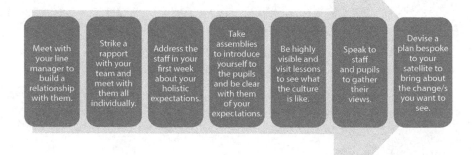

Meet with your line manager to build a relationship with them.

Strike a rapport with your team and meet with them all individually.

Address the staff in your first week about your holistic expectations.

Take assemblies to introduce yourself to the pupils and be clear with them of your expectations.

Be highly visible and visit lessons to see what the culture is like.

Speak to staff and pupils to gather their views.

Devise a plan bespoke to your satellite to bring about the change/s you want to see.

As a newly appointed middle leader, remember that people are looking to you for direction and leadership. You are now in charge, and failing to provide this will lose the support of people fairly swiftly.

Take your time to get to know your immediate team, to understand your satellite's context and to build relationships with both pupils and staff alike.

64: YOUR KINGDOM?

The relationship between the mothership and your satellite area of the school will have a bearing on how you run your year group, phase or subject. It is important, whatever this relationship is, that you are clear with the staff you manage about what your expectations are. First and foremost, you need to carefully consider these expectations for yourself. What is your vision and your halcyon dream/ideal for the area you are responsible for? If you do not know the answer to this, then you are going to struggle to articulate a vision to anyone else. This will then lead to confusion and ultimately, where there is confusion, this will transcend to the pupils and how they behave.

KEY CONSIDERATIONS

Ensure that you have a clear vision for your area of the school that is clearly defined and easy to understand and, importantly, that you have taken the views of your team to create this vision.	Clearly articulate your vision to the staff you are responsible for and to the pupils. All key stakeholders need to know what the expectations are within your area of the school.
Do not stray from the vision, values and ethos of the school. Even if the interrelationship between the mothership and your satellite is weak, you still need to uphold what the school stands for.	Ensure that you train, model and remodel your expectations so people can see what they look like, emulate them and make them a habitual part of their own expected norms.

WARNING

It can be natural as a subject leader to focus more of your energy and efforts on the academic bias of your curriculum design and intent. Do not forget that expectations, especially around behaviour, are just as important.

ADVICE

Do not assume that if you have presented something once to your staff that you do not need to revisit it. Staff, just like pupils, will need to be reminded and supported until your expectations become the established norm.

PS

65: LEADING AND MANAGING

As a middle leader you have to straddle being both a class teacher in its own right, a middle leader and, at times, a manager. Not only do you have to lead your satellite but you have to lead and manage the team of staff that work for you. Leadership is where you inspire people and bring them together, whereas managing is where you have to assert your authority and control. Both are needed at times, though leading is more likely to bring people with you. This is key with behaviour as well. You will need to both lead and manage the pupils that come through your satellite area of the school.

SOME CONSIDERATIONS

A key element is to decide on your style of leadership and management and what approach naturally fits your personality.	I would encourage you to be visible and a presence so you can support your team as much as is viably possible. You also need to be a visible presence in the eyes of the pupils if you are to establish yourself with them.
As a middle leader you need to be clear with the pupils what your expectations of them are and how they should behave in your subject area/phase/as part of your year group.	A huge part of your success as a middle leader will be built upon creating positive working relationships with your immediate team and with the pupils.

WARNING

As a middle leader, you cannot absolve yourself of responsibility for leading on and supporting staff with behaviour. To do so is to fail the staff who work under you and it will leave them feeling unsupported and lacking faith in your leadership.

ADVICE

As a middle leader, you need to consider carefully how you build your team and take professional responsibility for leading on behaviour within your satellite. You also need to ensure that you communicate regularly and consistently with your team so they know where they stand, what is expected of them and what the team's priorities are.

PS

66: TRAINING YOUR TEAM

As a middle leader you may be afforded year-team, subject-team or phase-team meetings. While the priorities of your satellite's immediate foci are important, you should also consider carefully how you train your team in behaviour and in your satellite-specific routines and norms. Your approaches should always dovetail and mirror the mothership's, but equally may need to be tweaked and/or amended to be bespoke to your area of the school. If you fail to do this, you cannot expect your team to know how to do things. You will also need to revisit and reboot your team from time to time. As with the mothership's approach you should think of it like this:

If you do not train your immediate team in your expectations, routines and norms, then who will? You will be leaving staff to guess what you want and your expectations will be assumed, not driven.

You need to consider carefully how you support and train new staff as they join your team, otherwise they may struggle in their role. New staff, be they new to the profession or the school, deserve your time and guidance if they are to succeed.

67: SAFEGUARDING

As a middle leader you have a role to play in safeguarding your immediate team. It is important that you support those staff under your wing, especially more naïve or inexperienced members of staff, to engage in professional working practices that will allow them to stay safe. Equally, as their line manager you need to be at hand, and I appreciate in the frantic rush of a bustling school day that it is a challenge to support a team member if they have had to deal with a safeguarding case that is traumatic for them. Staff will want your advice and support. As a middle leader you can (and I speak from personal experience) feel out of your depth here. So it is important that you can consult with your line manager. Equally, some middle leaders have significant pastoral responsibilities and you will find that you are very much at the forefront when children want to speak to someone about a concern.

CONSIDERATIONS

Create a safeguarding protocol for your team, in line with the school's policies, so all members of your team know what to do and what is expected.	Ensure that the meetings you chair have safeguarding as an agenda item so you can discuss safeguarding matters with your team and/or train your team where applicable and appropriate.
Train staff, especially if your role is pastoral, to look at attendance data carefully. Attendance data can often be utilised to identify potential safeguarding concerns.	Ensure that your own safeguarding training is in place, up to date and regularly refreshed. Speak to your line manager if you are anxious about your training lapsing.

WARNING

Do not assume, especially as a curriculum-based middle leader, that safeguarding has very little to do with you and that it is someone else's responsibility. Given your level of seniority, you have a key role to perform and need to serve as a means of support for your staff.

ADVICE

Make safeguarding part of your satellite's culture. The more frequently and regularly it is discussed, the less daunting it will become for you and your team. In time it will become part of the established cultural norm.

PS

68: CURRICULUM DESIGN

One of the overarching messages of this book is that good planning does not necessarily lead to good behaviour. However, with great systems in place, behaviour for learning can become flat or sterile if the planning and sequencing of the curriculum has not been carefully thought through. As a subject-based middle leader/phase leader, you have a lot of responsibility on your shoulders to ensure your curriculum is fit for purpose and that you have built in the teaching of behaviour. Here are some key considerations.

KEY CONSIDERATIONS

- **Why?** Do you know why your curriculum exists? Do you know why you have picked the topics and units that you have elected to teach?

- **Ethos aligned:** Is your curriculum in line with the school's ethos?

- **Vision and values aligned:** Does your curriculum support and allow for the development and teaching of the school's vision and values?

- **Character promotion:** Where does your curriculum domain seamlessly weave in the teaching and development of character?

- **Behaviour as a subject:** Where does your curriculum allow for the explicit teaching of behaviour and where are behavioural reboots built in?

- **Expectations:** Is the curriculum and its content sufficiently challenging to allow pupils to make progress, but does it also support, build on and develop their wider acquired knowledge?

- **Big Questions:** Have you considered the Big Questions and ideas that you want the pupils to know and how these questions manifest at a lesson-specific level?
- **Knowledge:** Have you considered the specific subject domain knowledge and subject domain skills you want the pupils to know and have learned both holistically and at a lesson-specific level?
- **Sequencing, interleaving and retrieval:** Have you carefully considered where these three key interlinking elements should reside and support learning?

WARNING

You must take the time to contemplate and subsequently plan out your curriculum so you can reinforce behavioural and learning-orientated expectations. Do not separate the two.

ADVICE

If you work with at least one other colleague then promote co-planning and the sharing of resources. Satellite teams should not operate as a group of islands; this is a poor use of time.

S

69: LEADING AND SUPPORTING A TEAM OF TUTORS

As a middle leader you may well have responsibility for a team of tutors. This is more likely to be the case in a secondary school, and those carrying a house or year group responsibility are more likely to have direct responsibility for this team of staff. It is really important to consider carefully the identity that your year group or house will carry. How do you want to be known? How do you want to be identified? What is your year group or house motto? As a subject-based middle leader, how will you support on this front? It may be that a set of tutors for a given year team come from a particular subject area. If so, how will you (assuming you are not a tutor yourself) support what is essentially your team as well? How will you work with the year or house leader if you are an academic subject lead?

SOME CONSIDERATIONS

Carefully consider how visible you will be and how you can ensure during tutor periods that you are a visible presence with your tutors.	Can you engineer a situation where your year group or house are located in the same geographical area of the school so you can easily access and support every tutor group?
Do you have a regular, short and sharp weekly meeting that is 15-20 minutes in length with your tutor team so you can discuss real-time issues as they arise, convey key messages that you need tutors to deliver and support your team?	How do you ensure that institutional messages are carefully delivered to your team and how do you ensure that they receive regular and timely training to perform their role?

WARNING

Do not assume that all staff within your team will automatically know how to be a tutor and do not assume that every tutor will know how to deliver the tutor-time curriculum (if there is one in place) both effectively and consistently. You need to work hard to support this.

ADVICE

If you do not have a structured approach to your tutor-time delivery and the way that your team of tutors operates, then I would seek to create one. I would also create a year or house code of conduct for the staff within your team, that outlines their role and responsibilities and your role and responsibilities so everyone is clear on the expectations that are set.

S

70: BIG LECTURES

You may wish to develop a programme of big lectures to the pupils that you serve. Big lectures are where you take two to three classes, half a year group or even a whole year group and teach them, almost university lecture style, in a big hall/space within your school. This is an alternative way of teaching, especially when you want to introduce a new topic, to consolidate a sequence of lessons or to support pupils with their revision in anticipation of a set of exams. In my experience pupils respond well to this approach, but only if you set the big lecture up appropriately. Therefore, your planning of a big lecture or series of big lectures is key.

SOME CONSIDERATIONS

Once you know where you want to position a big lecture within your sequence of learning, you need to consider carefully what you will deliver (in terms of knowledge) within the lecture itself.	You need to ensure that the space you are going to use is set up with singular exam-style desks, whiteboards for the pupils to use, appropriate stationery, a screen and a large whiteboard or, ideally, a visualiser.
Whichever member of staff delivers the lecture needs to consider their use of voice and how they project their voice within the accommodation being used.	You need more than one member of staff to run a big lecture en masse, and each person involved will need to have a clear role and function to perform.

WARNING

Prior to delivering a big lecture, especially if this is the first time you have ever engaged in this approach, you must be clear with the pupils what your expectations are and to rehearse these before commencing this approach. This should be done in normal lessons so pupils know what to expect, what the lecture's purpose is and why you are adopting this approach.

ADVICE

You will need to train your team of staff in the expectations, routines and norms first so they know what messages to convey to the pupils. Big lectures can serve as a fantastic CPD opportunity for staff whose subject knowledge may be less secure for a given topic. This is a chance to hear the most experienced member of a team flex their subject specialist expertise.

PS

71: OFSTED QUESTIONS

The following are possible Ofsted questions that middle leaders may be asked:

- What is the school's approach to behaviour?
- What is your role in supporting the school's approach?
- How has behaviour improved?
- How does the school tackle bullying and hate incidents?
- How does the school communicate with parents over behavioural issues?
- What training and support are you given as a middle leader?
- How do you support your team?
- How well do you understand the school's vision, values and ethos?
- How does the school support SEND children?
- Talk me through what happens when a pupil misbehaves in a lesson. What role do you play?
- Are staff supported?
- What training is given to all staff across the school?
- How are support staff trained?

WARNING

While ultimately your name is not on the Ofsted inspection report, you should not underestimate the role that you may well play in an inspection and, given you occupy a leadership position within the school, the overall level of responsibility that you carry.

ADVICE

Prior to any Ofsted inspection you should consider carefully both the types of questions that Ofsted can pose and your answers. These should be authentic and grounded in what you and your school actually do. Always remember that an inspectorate team will triangulate what you say with evidence from other key stakeholders.

72: SUPPORTING CHILDREN

It is really important that you never lose sight of why you are doing the job and undertaking the role that you do. You should never lose sight of the impact that your leadership and teaching has on the children. You should always remember that whatever approach you are taking is for the children. If you ignore how children will benefit or be supported by your actions, leadership and management, then you need to go back to the drawing board.

There are some key considerations for you regarding the strategies and approaches you can employ to support children, both with their learning and their behaviour, as follows.

SOME CONSIDERATIONS

Setting: You should weigh this approach up very carefully. Setting can work well in a school with a huge bandwidth of ability and less so where it is quite narrow, *but do not* set children due to their behaviour.	**SEND provision:** At a satellite level, what are you doing to support the needs of children with SEND? How are you training your team of staff to consider subject-specific strategies and approaches?
Collapsing groups to allow for team teaching: Sometimes bringing two classes together, where timetabling and space allows, can be a really powerful approach and will allow two staff to work as a duo to really support each other and the pupils. In some cases this can also be employed as an approach to support and train up a colleague.	**Direct Instruction:** Where do you take the time and consideration to train your team in methods of Direct Instruction (DI), which really allow them to develop a broader armoury of teaching approaches?

WARNING

Avoid, as best you can, being ideological about approaches. Sometimes there is a real need to set pupils by ability, for example, and at other times mixed-ability groups may work better. Keep an open mind here as every context is different.

ADVICE

Always carefully consider the needs of the pupils and staff who work in your team. Every year the state of play can vary and you must be professionally agile enough to respond to these changes.

SATELLITES: CONCLUDING THOUGHTS

'Middle leaders are the engine room of the school.'

Being a middle leader is a challenging role. Ultimately you are a leader. I have deliberately kept this section of the book concise because as a middle leader you have to juggle multiple balls. You really need to know and think carefully about the role of the mothership. You must also know how things operate at the micro level (i.e. in the classroom), because you straddle multiple camps as a middle leader. It is therefore important that you read both sections 1 and 3 of this book. You need to be able to think like a senior leader, operate as a middle leader and never lose sight of what it is to be a classroom teacher, while also considering the efficacy of your own classroom delivery. You need to be able to embody and blend together the needs of the mothership and the teachers under your wing, as well as spin your own set of middle leadership plates.

Whether you are an academic subject lead, a head of year/house or a phase lead, you need to carefully craft an identity for your satellite that mirrors and marries up with the mothership's ethos. Pupils need to know what you and your satellite stand for. They need to know what the year team or house group motto is. Identity is key to pupils and staff feeling that they have a sense of belonging and purpose. At all times you have to consider as a middle leader how you develop character, promote behaviour and model to the pupils and your team of staff what your expectations, values and norms are. There is no real end point to this. It has the potential to go on forever.

KEY TAKEAWAY POINTS

1. You have to be explicitly clear and train your team in your expectations, values and norms.
2. You are a vanguard of the mothership's vision, values and ethos.
3. Staff will look to you for support, coaching and mentoring and it is key to the success of your satellite that you provide this.
4. You must have a clear plan of action for your satellite to drive your vision.
5. It is critical that you are highly visible (obviously, teaching commitments permitting).

COMMON MISCONCEPTIONS

1. Behaviour is not your responsibility, especially as an academic subject lead.
2. The vision for driving change solely comes from SLT and middle leaders play no part in this.
3. You are not part of the leadership of the school.
4. The staff in your team should consume their own smoke, i.e. they should deal with behavioural issues themselves.
5. It is not the middle leader's responsibility to train their immediate team. All training should be provided by the mothership.

REFLECTIONS

Please use the following space, having read the satellite section, to write any key reflections or take-home points that you are considering or may action.

_____

_____

_____

_____

_____

_____

_____

_____

_____

_____

_____

_____

_____

_____

_____

SECTION 3:
THE MICRO LEVEL:
CLASS-BASED BEHAVIOUR STRATEGIES FOR TEACHERS

Teaching is taxing. Every day, staff are expected to deliver endless performances to children. It is theatre. It is panto. You have to know your stuff. You have to be on it. You have to command and control the room. You have to pre-empt misconceptions. It is an art form. Do not underestimate the role that you play, *but* you do not need behaviour to undermine your hard work and efforts.

INTRODUCTION

'Better than a thousand days of diligent study is one day with a great teacher.' Japanese proverb

The role and impact that a teacher has is often debated and discussed. There are those who argue and believe that teachers have a limited impact on the children that they serve, more so on their educational outcomes. I refute these claims. The impact a teacher has is almost beyond measure. I struggle to comprehend how a primary phase teacher, who sees the same children for six plus hours a day, has a limited impact on them. At a secondary level, where teachers are experts in one particular subject domain, I struggle to see how their precise and expert subject knowledge can fail to have a positive impact on the pupils that they teach. At GCSE and A-level teachers can and do have a major impact on the outcomes of the pupils that they serve. An inspiring teacher, with rich subject knowledge and a deep understanding of the exam specification, can have a demonstrable impact on outcomes. I see this year in, year out. I am not, and please do not confuse this, advocating using data to measure the impact a teacher can yield. I am, however, championing the role and importance of teachers. More alarming, with the Covid pandemic, have been wild claims that the world of IT can take over from the role that teachers play. This really demonstrates a huge lack of understanding that face-to-face teaching is where the magic happens. Nothing can truly replicate it and nothing can truly substitute for the human element and the relationships that are generated in a classroom. If you think otherwise, you are very naïve about the impact that teachers can have.

In a school setting, senior teams should serve as the school's defence. The head is the sweeper keeper and the senior team are the back four that defend the school, the staff and the pupils at all costs. Middle leaders almost serve as the box-to-box midfielder that runs up and down the pitch game after game after game. In a school setting, day after day, teachers, if you stay with this footballing analogy, perform an almost conflicting dual role. They are the defensive midfielder, who has to work tirelessly and do so much of the unseen work that allows the team to perform, but they are also the Roy of the Rovers of the school. They are the star. They are the ones who take the ball, make the magic happen and allow the team to win. Like it or not, teachers allow school improvement to happen. Yes – and I hugely believe this – a head who knows what they are doing makes a massive difference to a school. Ditto a senior team and a middle leader layer who are en pointe. But the classroom is where it all happens. This is where the game plan, the strategy and the intent underpinning your curricular design come into play. The enacted curriculum is ultimately what will make or break your school improvement strategy. If you get this right, if the school gets it right and, importantly, if the teachers get it right, then it is game on. If not, you are in trouble.

There is one key factor though, no matter how strong, centrally planned, carefully crafted and orchestrated the school system is, that will make or break teachers and that is behaviour. Teachers need to have a toolkit of strategies in their professional armoury that they can call upon to pre-empt, respond to and deal with behaviour in their classroom settings. Children ultimately know which teachers take behaviour seriously and which do not. If I were to ask you, 'Who was your favourite teacher and why?' I imagine the responses would broadly encapsulate a teacher who knew their stuff, cared about you, built relationships and who was firm but fair. This section of the book looks at a repertoire of strategies that class-based teachers can trial, hone, refine and call upon to make their class delivery all the better. I hope it supports all teachers and makes you think.

73: CURATING YOUR CLASSROOM CULTURE

As a teacher you are responsible for the behaviour in your classroom and the culture of learning that takes place within your lessons. It is critically important that you adhere to your school's behaviour policy and expectations. It is also vitally important that your approach ties in with the school's ethos, vision and values. Whatever your classroom expectations and rules may be, there are a number of key factors that are really important when curating your class culture, as follows:

- Remember to teach behaviour to your pupils as part of your overall lesson delivery.
- Front-load your expectations.
- Repeat your expectations.
- Always follow through with pupils where you have told them something will happen as a consequence of their actions.
- It is not a weakness to tactically ignore a pupil who is misbehaving but you must tactically find a point to address the behaviour.
- Never ignore poor behaviour.
- Never condone rudeness as this ultimately undermines you as the teacher.
- Adopt a positive mindset.
- Ensure that you plan lessons to platform the content, so the content becomes the engager, but ensure your lessons are appropriately challenging and keep your pupils busy.

WARNING

Irrespective of how strong a school's behaviour system and approach is, you still have to enact, curate and encourage positive behaviour in your classroom.

ADVICE

Nip all issues in the bud. Do not adopt the view that in ignoring an issue it will go away. If you ignore poor behaviour and do not follow through and address it, then this behaviour will be repeated. You ignoring it essentially says it is okay. Think to yourself, you permit what you promote and you promote what you permit.

PS

74: PLANNING FOR POSITIVE BEHAVIOUR

As a teacher, lesson planning is important. No one disputes that. I do, however, strongly advocate collaborative and joint lesson planning so that there is a really consistent approach to lesson delivery. I also appreciate that in smaller settings, where there is only one teacher teaching a year group or a subject, that this can be a huge challenge unless there is a strong external network in place. One thing teachers should do though is plan for behaviour. While I would never dispute the relevancy of lesson material, subject knowledge and the content that you are going to teach, it is also critical that you plan for positive behaviour. For less experienced teachers, I would argue that as much, if not more time, needs to go into considering how you plan for the behaviours that you want. I would go so far as to say that nothing should be left to chance; everything should be meticulously scripted and rehearsed. If you want the enacted curriculum and, importantly, the content to take centre stage, then you cannot afford for poor behaviour to ambush, derail or undermine your lesson.

SOME KEY QUESTIONS FOR YOUR CONSIDERATION

- What do you define positive behaviour as?
- What are your lines in the sand?
- How many warnings will you give before issuing a sanction?
- What do you want the social norm to be in your classroom?
- How do you want your pupils to enter your classroom?
- How do you want your classroom laid out?
- How do you want the furniture in your classroom to be arranged?
- Where do you want the pupils to sit?
- Where is the board in relation to the pupils?

- Will you circulate the room, stand at the front, sit at a desk or something else?
- Do you want pupils to stand at their desks and wait for permission to be seated or will you allow them to instantly sit as they enter the room?
- How do you want the pupils to transition from one activity to the next?
- What are your views on punctuality to your lessons?
- What emphasis will you place on pupil attire?
- What do you want to do regarding homework?
- Do you want your pupils to arrive equipped to your lessons or will you provide them with all that they need?
- How do you want pupils to answer questions? Do you want pupils to put their hands up?
- How will you end your lessons?
- How do you want the pupils to exit your classroom?
- How quickly do you want pupils to get changed if required?
- How do you want your pupils to conduct practical work, such as experiments?
- How will you explain the health and safety around using a piece of equipment, again, where applicable?
- How do you want pupils to present their work?
- How many displays do you want in your classroom? What will you have displayed?

WARNING

If you fail to adequately and adeptly plan for behaviour and assume that it will just happen, then you are likely to encounter problems within your lessons from the word go.

ADVICE

Look at the approaches employed by other members of staff in their lessons. While you do not want to emulate blow for blow how other teachers teach, it is worth watching how other staff command their classroom. Always adhere to the expectations and parameters as laid out in the whole-school behaviour policy.

PS

75: KNOWING YOUR PUPILS

It is really important that you know the pupils in your class. While this may seem a rather obvious point to make, it is one that can often be overlooked. The prior knowledge and data that you have on the pupils you are teaching is invaluable. It can help to inform the personalised support that you may give to pupils, how you speak to certain pupils and, where necessary, the reasonable adjustments that you put into place, all of which can help you to manage the pupils more effectively and proactively limit the number of behavioural issues that you face.

KEY INFORMATION TO CONSIDER

SEND profiles: It is key that you immerse yourself in the SEND profiles of any pupils in your class that have a special educational need. How you cater for their individualised needs and make reasonable adjustments in your lessons is important.	**Pupil profiles:** Most schools record important information about pupils on an information management system. Make sure you take the time to read up on the children that you teach to check if there are any pre-conditions that you need to have in place, if there is a set way in which you should speak to them, so as not to antagonise them, or if you need support should it be required.
Academic data: You should consider the academic data your school has available on your class's past performance to ascertain where there may be gaps in pupil learning and then consider carefully how to bridge those gaps so pupils can access the curriculum.	**Information from families/previous schools:** Speaking to families or a child's previous school as they transition to you can help you to consider carefully the approaches that you employ with the pupils in front of you.

WARNING

I am not suggesting you compromise your standards and expectations but there are times where a one-size approach will not fit all and you will have to adopt a more bespoke, personalised approach. Being professionally agile is vital to your success.

ADVICE

Avoid stereotyping pupils and assuming that because a pupil offers few verbal contributions in class that they may be less able. They may possess less acquired knowledge than their peers and the challenge for you as the teacher will be to bring pupil X up to speed with their classmates.

PS

76: COGNITIVE LOAD

While this book is not a book that focuses on cognitive load or cognitive theory, it would be remiss when considering behaviour not to touch on it. How the human brain works and how children learn can have a real impact on how they behave in our lessons. It is therefore important to consider arming yourself with strategies and approaches that help support and address cognitive load. Dylan Wiliam has described cognitive load as 'the single most important thing for teachers to know'.[9] It is important to note that pupils having to remember routines and norms is a cognitive load in itself, so the simpler and more embedded your systems are, the lower the load, therefore freeing up more space for curriculum learning. If pupils have to guess what a teacher wants, that adds to their cognitive load.

SOME KEY APPROACHES

Ensure lessons are tailored to the existing knowledge and skill base that the pupils possess.	Employ the use of worked examples to teach the pupils the knowledge and disciplinary skills that they need.
Introduce problem solving and independent approaches to lessons once pupils are confident and, importantly, proficient with the knowledge.	Ensure that you teach the precise information the pupils need to know and cut out what is not essential or necessary.
Present information to your pupils both visually and orally, especially when the information is complex.	Model success to the pupils so they know what they are striving for.

WARNING

Carefully consider the number of displays that you have in your classroom and how visually loud they are. If there are too many on display this can result in cognitive overload.

ADVICE

It's important to always consider employing strategies that reduce the overall load on a pupil's working memory so as to maximise learning. Keeping your class calm and orderly is also essential.

PS

77: BUILDING POSITIVE RELATIONSHIPS

It is really important that you build a set of positive and professional working relationships with the pupils that you teach. Relationships are ultimately everything within teaching and why, in some regards, teaching is as much an art as it can be described as a science (but that is a different debate). The relationships that you strike up with the pupils you teach will tell them everything that they need to know about you as their teacher. Children are more likely to work hard for a teacher that they buy into, whether we like it or not. Differing educational theorists give different badges or titles to key approaches that we can take. Doug Lemov defines the relationship that we should seek to create as Warm/Strict.[10] Bill Rogers calls it Warm Assertiveness.[11] Some people cite firm but fair. I personally think all of these labels have a similar meaning and, as I stated earlier in this book, I would refer to a teacher as a 'children's champion'. Namely, you need clear boundaries, but you need to give some warmth, compassion and kindness to your pupils.

The following diagram outlines some key considerations in how to be a children's champion for you to ponder over.

WARNING

While there should be an assumed level of respect that is given to teachers (and I do firmly believe this), there also has to be a realisation that people are more respectful, polite, courteous and, ultimately, will work harder for people that they buy into. Relationships are crucial.

ADVICE

You need to define for yourself the type of teacher that you want to be and how you want to convey yourself to the children that you serve.

PS

78: YOUR CLASSROOM, YOUR RULES/ EXPECTATIONS

It is really important to consider the rules and/or expectations that you want to see demonstrated in your classroom. Irrespective of how strong the level of influence is from the mothership to your classroom setting, there is still a very strong need for every teacher to assert their own set of expectations. As a teacher you need to clearly define these and, more importantly, take the time to communicate, explicitly explain and train your pupils in these expectations. If your expectations are a mystery to the pupils then you cannot expect them to behave and respond to you in the manner that you want. Your lessons will become a challenge. Marzano,[12] a behavioural educationalist, cites that classrooms should be based on four key rules, namely:

- Quiet when the teacher is talking.
- We follow directions right away.
- We let others get on with their work.
- We respect each other.

SOME KEY CONSIDERATIONS

Have your expectations/rules clearly displayed in your classroom.	Ensure your expectations are simple, straightforward and easy to understand.
Avoid using ambiguous or grey language. For example, 'quiet' has no real clear meaning.	Consider carefully how you explain and train your pupils in your expectations.

WARNING

It is tempting to have lots of rules and expectations but a fundamental question to consider is, will the pupils remember them? Pupils are likely to remember three main expectations but if you have 10 expectations then it is unlikely that pupils will be able to recall these.

ADVICE

It is really important that you train your pupils to not only know and understand what you want but also to remember what you want from one lesson to the next and from one day to the next.

PS

79: KNOW WHAT YOU WANT

As a classroom teacher, it is critical that you know what sort of classroom-based culture you want to see. At least 90% of your time as a full-time class teacher, with no area of responsibility, will be based in a classroom. You do not want this time to be unpleasant, undermined by poor behaviour and low-level disruption, and you do not want to find that you cannot do your core job, namely to teach.

It is critical that you do the following three things:

1. Know what culture you want.

2. Communicate this culture effectively.

3. Teach that culture and maintain that culture.

WARNING

If you do not know what you want your classroom environment to be like, then who will? You cannot leave this to chance or simply assume that it will be crafted for you.

ADVICE

Take the time to map out how you want your classroom to operate. Taking the time to consider this is just as important as planning lesson resources or enhancing your subject knowledge.

80: HEALTH AND SAFETY AND USING THE ROOM

If you teach a practical subject, you really need to think your health and safety protocols through carefully. Subjects such as science, art, PE, dance, drama, design technology, food technology and music (to name but a few) all have important approaches to health and safety that have to be adhered to, many of which are statutory. It is important if you teach these subjects to think carefully about how you front-load your expectations, model them explicitly and check continually with the pupils for their understanding.

SOME CONSIDERATIONS

Changing room facilities: You need to carefully consider how these are supervised when pupils are getting changed. You cannot leave them unattended.	**Practical safety equipment (goggles, aprons, etc.):** You must ensure that your classroom is equipped with these and pupils know how to use the equipment safely.
Dangerous equipment: For example, when using lathes, Bunsen burners, cookers, scissors, climbing equipment, etc., you must explicitly articulate to pupils how to use these pieces of equipment and ensure that the pupils are supervised at all times.	**Handing out equipment:** Always count out and count in equipment so no pupil leaves your classroom with a piece of equipment that they should not be carrying. Think here about scissors and knives.
Demonstration areas: Having a clear space in your classroom set up to demonstrate is key, but you also need to ensure that the pupils are suitably distanced from you if you are undertaking an experiment. PE teachers, as an example, need to consider carefully how they divide their indoor or outdoor space to ensure pupils can watch a demonstration and then practise.	**Pupils' own safety equipment:** Some subjects will require pupils to have their own safety equipment. It is important that the expectations around this equipment are well communicated to families and, come your lesson, you have spare safety equipment to hand for those pupils who may have forgotten to bring it (assuming the school does not provide it).

WARNING

Never be complacent about health and safety and never assume pupils know. Teaching a practical subject requires endless checking for understanding.

ADVICE

You will need to devote lesson time to explicitly explaining your expectations and to modelling how practical aspects of the lesson work so pupils are safe at all times. This will require you to have scripted and rehearsed your approach.

PS

81: CLASSROOM ASSISTANTS/TEACHING ASSISTANTS

At times there may be another adult in your classroom setting. They may be a teaching assistant, attached to a particular pupil, or a classroom assistant whose role is to support you and the children that you are teaching. These additional adults can add another positive dimension to your lessons and to your teaching but equally, if your collective communication is poor, then the relationship can become fractious and undermine your approach. It is therefore important to work together as a team to aid one another with lesson delivery.

The following offers some advice for working with classroom/teaching assistants.

SOME TIPS

Meet with the assistant and establish your joint classroom expectations and take the time to ask them how they are hoping to support you and the children, and how you can support them.	Before a new unit of work commences take the time to meet with the assistant to share the curriculum vision and plan for the term ahead so they know what both your roles are, what the content is and what the overall plan is.
Create a shared language for learning and behaviour, with a clear understanding that you are both in charge of the class, though ultimately the teacher is accountable. Also, be clear with each other that you will never publicly (in front of the pupils) undermine one another.	Discuss the children in the class at length, considering any specific and bespoke needs that may need supporting.

WARNING

The working relationship you forge with any class- or teaching-based assistant is critical to the success of your lessons.

ADVICE

You need to be clear from the outset that the class/teaching assistant must address behavioural issues that you do not permit or promote, or that counter the school's approach and expectations. It is also wise to establish regular meetings with this additional adult so the channels of communication remain true and strong.

82: TEACHING CHARACTER

Teachers have a role to play in the development and teaching of character. Promoting and teaching pupils key virtues which in turn translate into actions, habits and norms is critical to supporting the collective drive for a culture, climate and ethos of positive behaviour. If you fail to do this, you will inadvertently undermine the ethos and climate for learning that you want to see your pupils demonstrate.

HOW CAN YOU SUPPORT CHARACTER DEVELOPMENT?

Consider carefully how you model the behaviour, manners, virtues and language that you want to see in your pupils.	Build in opportunities that are genuine and authentic to reinforce your school's values, ethos and norms.
Where applicable, present moral virtue discussions with your class. This could be through academic reading, stories, case studies or problem solving. This allows pupils to consider issues and how best to approach them.	Platform where pupils display positive acts of character in your lessons and promote opportunities for pupils to work in a manner that allows them to develop their overall levels of oracy.

WARNING

Be wary of turning character into an artificial bolt-on. It needs to be neatly embedded into your delivery so it is part and parcel of what you do. It should formulate part of your established norm within lessons.

ADVICE

When you plan and sequence your curriculum you should consider where opportunities reside for you to explicitly and implicitly teach the development of character to your pupils.

PS

83: A SIMPLE APPROACH TO LESSONS

Keeping your approach to lessons simple, especially at the start of your lesson, can make a huge difference to your pupils. If there is a consistent and well-rehearsed routine to the start of your lessons, then pupils will swiftly realise that they are expected to arrive at your lessons promptly and engage with the learning straight away. This reduces the scope for pupils to misbehave and enhances the overall amount of learning time you can capitalise on.

A SUGGESTED APPROACH

The following serves purely as an example of an approach that you could adopt.

1. Meet and greet your class at the door of your classroom, with a warm and positive welcome – *this sets the tone for the lesson from the off and supports you to build relationships.*

2. As pupils enter the classroom they should engage with a 'Do Now' or 'Engage' task. As you refine your teaching, you may wish to adopt a retrieval practice starter, which serves as a settler – *the importance here is that no time is wasted and that pupils enter your room knowing that they are there to learn.*

3. Pupils then peer or self-mark their starter task – *this supports you with workload and provides pupils with instant feedback.*

4. Present the context for the lesson – *this essentially serves as the 'why', so pupils understand what they are learning, why and how it fits into the bigger picture.*

5. Hang the lesson against a Big Question (for example, 'How significant was the Wall Street Crash in supporting Hitler to come to power in 1933?') – *the use of a Big Question serves a number of purposes. It serves as a clear lesson/series of lesson headers for pupils and their work, it provides a clear focus for your lesson, pupils should work towards answering the Big Question and it provides a framework that gives the disciplinary knowledge a greater sense of purpose and meaning.*

6. Then deliver in a manner relevant to your subject – *it is important to recognise that every subject discipline requires a potentially different methodology of delivery.*

WARNING

A huge misconception is that clear routines for learning hinder teacher freedom and creativity. They do the reverse. They allow teachers to maximise learning, settle classes swiftly and ensure no time is wasted.

ADVICE

I would wholeheartedly recommend taking the time to map out, plan and then rehearse your lesson routines before you air them live with your pupils.

PS

84: ROUTINES FOR LEARNING

Routines for learning are key. They define everything about you, your classroom setting, your expectations and the learning that will or will not take place in your lessons. As Doug Lemov[13] stated, 'Perhaps the single most powerful way to bring efficiency, focus and rigour to a classroom is by installing strong procedures and routines.' Essentially, routines are a behaviour that you want to see in your lessons. They are standardised by you and carried out by the pupils until they are habitual. Once a routine becomes habitual it is embedded into the memory of your pupils and lessons become more efficient, with commands carried out on cue. The following diagram is a useful visual when considering routines:

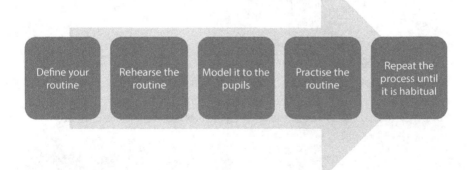

WARNING

Some people see routines as being far too prescriptive, constricting the overall flow of a lesson. This is a mistaken viewpoint. Clear routines liberate you so you can teach your lessons and maximise their efficiency.

ADVICE

If you want to see routines for learning in action, visit an EYFS teacher and see how they operate. They leave nothing to chance and narrate every single expectation to create a safe environment where the children in their care are absolutely certain of the expectations set.

PS

85: FRONT-LOAD YOUR EXPECTATIONS

It is really important that from the onset with a new class you are clear about the expectations that you want, expect and insist on. It is key that you front-load these fairly swiftly so pupils know precisely what to expect, when and how. However, I would advocate that you carefully and skilfully weave your expectations into your class delivery and routinely build from one lesson to the next the standard you both expect and want. There is a real danger that at the start of a new academic year, especially in a secondary setting, pupils can end up in relentless and endless 30-60 minute lectures about teacher expectations that end up switching pupils off. I personally feel you will have more impact with your pupils if you get straight into the learning but narrate the expectations as you transition within your lessons, ensuring that you build from one lesson to the next.

HOW TO FRONT-LOAD YOUR EXPECTATIONS

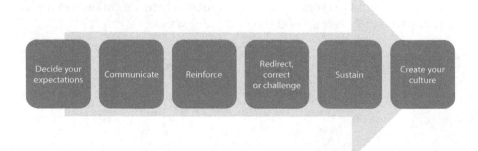

WARNING

Failing to explicitly front-load your expectations will cause you more work later. You are likely to encounter more problems as you work with your class/classes.

ADVICE

Consider carefully how you can narrate, model and train your class/ classes in your expectations without compromising the content and their learning.

PS

86: CONSEQUENCE OR CORRECTION?

At multiple points in this book I have promoted you to use the behaviour system that is in place within your school. Failing to do so will ultimately cause you more issues than not. However, as part of your behavioural toolkit, you should also consider carefully when to employ the use of a consequence and when to use a correction. If a pupil is publicly rude to you, for example, then you should never condone it or leave this unresolved. However – and I am not trying to promote inconsistency in practice – there may be times where a correction in the here and now is more powerful than consequence, but the consequence may need to be issued at a more discreet moment in the lesson. Equally, you may have a pupil who has just suffered a major bereavement or has significant safeguarding issues surrounding them; would their poor behavioural choices be better served with a correction?

POINTS TO CONSIDER

It is worth considering carefully situations and circumstances where you feel a correction would be more beneficial than a punitive sanction.	Script how you would narrate your correction, even if it is only in your head.
Contemplate what your next step will be if your attempt at correcting a pupil's behaviour fails to have the impact you intended.	Never leave yourself in a position where you have unwittingly undermined yourself in the eyes of the pupils.

WARNING

Do not continually shift between consequences and corrections, especially where differing pupils display the same behaviour but are issued with a differing consequence. This can breed a sense that you are inconsistent among the pupils or that you have personal favourites. This is a dangerous position.

ADVICE

Sometimes it is necessary to narrate to the other pupils in a class that you have had to correct a pupil's behaviour rather than sanction it due to difficult and challenging personal circumstances for the pupil. Never state what those issues actually are, but sometimes adopting this approach can help pupils to understand what may look like an inconsistency.

PS

87: HOW MANY WARNINGS?

Should a teacher employ the use of consequences or corrections? This question hugely divides opinions. If you take no prisoners and instantly jump to the use of sanctions, it could be deemed that you are being extreme and employing a zero-tolerance approach. On the other hand, some may deem that you have a no-nonsense approach and that you are firmly within your rights to act swiftly at the slightest sign of poor behaviour. Some will cite that it is your professional duty to act in this manner and that such an approach firmly builds upon the expectations as laid out in the teacher standards. Some people will cite that you may break relationships with pupils in being too quick to sanction, whereas other people will cite that you are more likely to earn the respect of those pupils who want to learn. A big question is the number of warnings that you employ.

HOW MANY WARNINGS?

A common approach is three strikes and you are sanctioned or you are removed. Warning one may be a look or a verbal reprimand. Warning two may be to write a pupil's name on the board. Warning three may be to move a pupil within the context of the classroom to a different seat. In theory this approach sounds reasonable, fair and proportionate. However, I want you to think carefully about the implications of this type of approach. If you have a class of 30 pupils who all misbehave during the course of the lesson, then you could find yourself in a very difficult and tiring position. For example, if you are employing a three-warning approach then you could find in any given lesson you are issuing 90 warnings to 30 pupils before anything happens. Over the course of a five-lesson day, you could be issuing 450 warnings before anything happens. I appreciate that this is potentially an extreme extrapolation to exemplify a point but this is the possible issue with a three-warning approach.

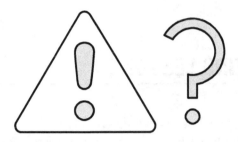

WARNING

Always carefully consider the unintended consequences of your behavioural approach and the sustainability of any approach that you decide to employ.

ADVICE

Ensure your behavioural approach or warning system does not lead to an intolerable and cumbersome workload issue for you. Also ensure that the approach you employ is both in keeping with the school's policy and allows you to nip issues in the bud swiftly.

S

88: STARTING LESSONS

How you start your lesson tells the pupils a lot about what to expect for the duration of that lesson. How you consistently and consecutively commence your lessons tells the pupils a lot about you, your expectations, your values, and your established and expected norms. It also tells them what is and what is not permissible. The more certainty, consistency and continuity you can give them, the better. How a lesson begins will define the entire ebb and flow of the lesson itself. If the first 10-15 minutes is wasted settling the class, taking the register and copying down learning objectives, then how much learning can you claim, with confidence, has actually occurred? I have seen all too many lessons commence with pupils arriving in a rabble, sitting down and waiting for the teacher, then the teacher spends what appears to be an inordinate amount of finite lesson time settling the class, only then to take a register, which does not serve as an effective lesson settler.

HOW TO START A LESSON

Meet and greet pupils at the door of your classroom, with one foot in the corridor and one foot in the classroom.	As pupils enter the classroom welcome each pupil, ideally using their name. Narrate that it is going to be a positive lesson.
Pupils should engage in a 'Do Now' or 'Engage' task, ideally retrieval in nature, so that no learning or lesson time is wasted. This should become an expected norm.	Go over the initial activity with the pupils and then present the context of the lesson to the class.

WARNING

Do not overcomplicate the start to your lesson. Pupils succeed most where there is certainty. Pupils are more likely to positively engage and respond where they know what to expect and where there is an established norm.

ADVICE

Once you know your class you can take a lesson register without formally calling out pupil names. Always consider, carefully, how much time you actually have with a class and how much learning time is lost by lower-order activities that do not support learning.

89: BIG QUESTIONS

If lessons are to be successful and pupils are going to know what they are doing, why, and what the overall purpose of the lesson is, then I would encourage you to use a Big Question to frame your lesson or sequence of lessons around. Pupils are less likely to misbehave and more likely to switch on if they know what the purpose of your lesson is. The idea underpinning a Big Question is that the question is generated from the disciplinary knowledge that you are seeking to teach your class. It serves as a framework upon which to hang all of the disciplinary knowledge you are encountering and teaching in a lesson, or lesson sequence.

EXAMPLES OF BIG QUESTIONS

- How did Hitler use the Treaty of Versailles as an ideological tool to gather support for his policies?
- What is supply and demand?
- Why do Christians celebrate Christmas?
- How does a smash force your opponent to make errors in badminton?
- How does the Pythagoras theorem work?
- What role does Edna play in *An Inspector Calls*?
- How does photosynthesis work?

WARNING

Do not make your Big Questions complicated, otherwise pupils will struggle to understand them.

ADVICE

If you carefully craft your Big Questions, they will add more meaning to your lessons and bring about a clever interplay between the core and the hinterland.

S

90: COMMAND THE ROOM

It is really important to be clear from the outset when your pupils enter your classroom that it is your classroom, not theirs. You are the teacher in charge. You are the expert. You are the one responsible. It is your room, your lesson to share with them and you are the teacher. If you fail to assert yourself professionally on your class, then you are sending out all the wrong messages to the pupils who are under your duty of care. They will feel that they own the room and can take charge over you. This is where the balance goes wrong and lessons can fall apart.

HOW TO COMMAND THE ROOM

I would heartily recommend standing at the door of your classroom, with one foot in and one foot out of the door, at the start of any key transition point.	Welcome your pupils. Adopt phrases such as 'Good morning Mr X, it is lovely to see you,' 'I know you are going to give me 100% today,' or 'I know you are going to show me your best.' From the outset you are warm and welcoming, but also saying to your pupils, 'You are here to work.'
A key advantage in standing at the doorway is that you are saying this is your space, your room and to go past you the pupil has to engage with you.	If a pupil happens to be taller than you, then the chances are they will make themselves smaller as they enter your room to get past you in the doorway. This reminds the pupil that you, the teacher, are in charge.

WARNING

Do not allow pupils to assume or believe that the classroom belongs to them. If you do, you could find very quickly that you are playing second fiddle to them.

ADVICE

Do not underestimate the importance of commanding your classroom and establishing from the off that it is your classroom.

PS

91: THE NATURAL STATE

It is really important that you clearly define the natural state within your classroom environment. What I mean by this term is how you want your lessons to operate and function and how you want the pupils to work. The natural state is essentially your go-to modus operandi for certain activities or periods of the lesson.

THE NATURAL STATE: CONSIDERATIONS

Written work: When you have asked your pupils to write an extended piece of work, they really should be working on their own and, arguably, in silence. When you want the class to work like this you need to frame it with total clarity over your expectations, so pupils know how long they are working for and that silence means silence.	**Classroom questioning:** You need to be very clear with your class when you engage in a whole-class questioning activity what the parameters are. I would argue that pupils should be sat in silence, actively listening and ready at all times to engage with the question-and-answer session.
Think-Pair-Share: There is a more detailed summary of this approach in this book, but you need to carefully consider how you orchestrate an approach like this.	**Group work:** If you are going to engage your class in group work, then you need to explicitly outline the parameters, expectations, time frames and roles that every member of the class will play.

WARNING

If you do not explicitly define and narrate to your pupils what the natural state looks like in your lessons, then do not be surprised when they do not behave in a manner that you expect.

ADVICE

It is important that you are clear in your own mind what your expectations are as you move your lesson from one phase to the next. Do keep in mind that you cannot expect a class to work in total silence for a full lesson, every lesson. This is actually quite an unhealthy approach.

92: POSITIVE FRAMING

Positive framing is an important approach to teaching. This is where the teacher is explicitly positive about the lesson, about what the pupils can achieve and what they can do. Throughout the course of the lesson, the teacher will narrate the positives, focus on pupil successes and depersonalise any issues that may arise.

POSITIVE FRAMING APPROACHES

Open your lesson by narrating a positive. For example, 'Today we are going to attempt some challenging work but I know you are more than capable of dealing with it.'	Adopt a frame of mind where you are always assuming the best, even if the previous lesson was unsuccessful. You should live in the here and now with your pupils and not dwell negatively on previous lessons.
Always narrate the positives when pupils are interacting with you and offering answers, even if their answers are incorrect. Positive framing helps to build their confidence in the content, in you and their ability and capacity to learn.	Where a pupil does something wrong or gets something wrong, depersonalise it.

WARNING

If you make a pupil's mistakes or poor behavioural choices personal, then you will begin to formulate negative relationships with your class/classes and your frame of mind can easily become very negative towards a class.

ADVICE

Take the view that every lesson presents a new beginning and a new opportunity with your pupils. Positive framing, both for you and them, can have a hugely positive and positively demonstrable impact on the flow of your lessons and the learning that takes place.

PS

93: I/WE/YOU

I/we/you is a fantastic teaching approach that can be applied as much to behaviour as it can be to modelling an activity or engaging a class in choral chanting. Here is how you can use I/we/you with a class when considering behaviour:

I do: This is where you demonstrate to the class the particular behaviour that you want them to engage in. This step is critical otherwise your pupils will not know what the expectations are.

We do: This is where you ask the class to practise the expectation as a collective. This is a much lower-stakes way of rehearsing something so you are not platforming pupil mistakes. It also allows you to check that the class can/cannot do what you want. You need to perform 'we do' three to five times at a minimum.

You do: This is where you ask pupils to practise the behaviour on their own or you pick pupils randomly and ask them to demonstrate so you can check for understanding.

WARNING

The first stage of this process is critical and without it your entire approach to teaching the behaviour or routine that you want will fall flat on its face.

ADVICE

Always take the time to consider and be able to narrate why you are asking the class to do something. Pre-empt pupils asking you the 'why' question and build it in as part of your initial explanation and narrative.

PS

94: EVERYONE PARTICIPATES

Your expectations around whole-class participation are key. If you want every member of your class to know a key piece of disciplinary knowledge, then you need to ensure that they say it out loud and that you question every single pupil so no one avoids contributing orally. In terms of your overall planning, this is less challenging than you may think. In terms of lesson delivery, the aim is to ensure that 100% of your class are involved and that every pupil speaks. The aim of an approach like this is to build pupil confidence. The more confident pupils are the more likely they are to engage with the curriculum.

HOW TO ENSURE EVERYONE PARTICIPATES

1. Clearly define the disciplinary knowledge that you want the pupils to know. For example, if you need all of your class to know that the area of a triangle is length × height divided by 2, then you need to narrate this to the class.
2. Get all of the pupils to verbally articulate how the area of a triangle is calculated.
3. Play games with this. Ask one side of the room to say how the area of a triangle is calculated out loud, then the other half of the room. Do it by rows or sections of the room.
4. Check every single pupil knows by asking every pupil, one at a time, to say the formula out loud.

WARNING

Do not settle for one or two pupils answering or articulating information to the rest of the group. How do you know all your pupils are clear?

ADVICE

With any verbal contribution that pupils offer always be positive about pupil responses, and when a pupil offers the wrong answer, come back to them to check for their understanding.

S

95: TRACKING THE TEXT

When you engage the class in a whole-class reading activity, how do you truly know that they are engaged with the text? How do you know that the pupils are not simply looking blankly at the page? A strategy you may wish to employ that will allow you to keep a closer tab on whether pupils are following the text or not, is tracking the text.

HOW DOES TRACKING THE TEXT WORK?

1. Firstly, you need to equip every pupil with a ruler.	2. You ask pupils to place their rulers on the first line of the text that you are going to read together as a class.
3. You then tell the class to be ready to track the text on line 1 in 3, 2, 1...	4. Pupils should then follow the text (tracking it) with their ruler and the text flat on their table.

WARNING

Be mindful that even when you engage in an activity like tracking the text pupils can still appear to be vacant. You will need to question the pupils and check for understanding as you work your way through the text.

ADVICE

While I would always advocate that the teacher should read out loud to their class, you need to ensure that the pupils are actively engaged and with you. At random you may wish to ask a pupil to read a sentence/ extract and mix this up to ensure all pupils are engaged with the learning.

PS

96: COLD CALLING

This approach is spoken about in detail by Doug Lemov in *Teach Like a Champion*.[14] In summary, this approach is highly effective. This is where you call on the pupils to answer a question irrespective of whether they have their hands up. As the teacher you ask a question and then call on the pupil who you want to answer it. This approach allows you to check for understanding effectively and systematically. It also allows you to distribute verbal answers across the room more broadly and evenly and it signals to the pupils that they are likely to be called upon to participate and should therefore engage in the work that is set.

KEY PRINCIPLES

You should make Cold Calling an embedded part of your lesson routine so pupils expect it.	It should be executed systematically, with everyone involved. There should be no excuses.
You must keep your approach positive, regardless of whether an answer is incorrect or not.	Ensure that the questions you employ are small in nature and can be distributed evenly across the room.

WARNING

If a pupil is unable to answer the question, which can happen, move away from them so as not to platform what they don't know, but do come back to them once the answer has been articulated by another pupil so you can check that they do now know it.

ADVICE

Ensure that when you engage in Cold Calling you are drawing on prior knowledge that you have already taught the class, otherwise the chances are the pupils will be unlikely to know the answer.

PS

97: SIMPLE LANGUAGE AND INSTRUCTIONS

It is important that the language and instructions that you give to your pupils are simple. The more complex, verbose and tricky your instructions and language are, the more chance you will lose your pupils.

Consider the following key points:

- Is the language that you use and the instruction that you have given specific?
- Have you given a clear set of instructions that are easy to understand?
- Do the pupils know and understand the words that you have used?
- Have you given the pupils a concrete example of what your instruction looks like so they can visualise and know what to do?
- Have you modelled the instruction so the pupils have seen it in action?
- After issuing an instruction, have you checked for understanding? In other words, have you asked pupils to clarify back to you what is expected of them?

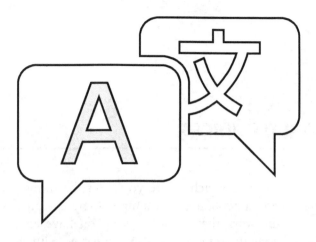

WARNING

If you issue instructions that are complex and difficult to comprehend, then the chances are your pupils will not understand what is expected of them and this can result in them misbehaving.

ADVICE

It is important to script and rehearse routine class instructions so they become habitual for you and you are not having to constantly think about how you issue them to your pupils in a lesson setting. You should always consider your own cognitive load as this will have an impact on your effectiveness.

98: CLOSED CHOICES

Closed choices is an approach where you limit the number of options that are available to a pupil. So, for example, there is a pupil who is not engaging with the work that has been set. You have already tried to positively encourage the pupil in question to get on with the work. You have asked them if they understand the task, if they need any help and you have tried to redirect them to the learning. At all junctures the pupil has responded with 'No, I'm fine' but the pupil is still not engaging. The number of options open to you becomes somewhat limited. It may be that at this stage you – in terms of how you deal with this – are going to engage in a closed choice.

NARRATING A CLOSED CHOICE

Having politely and professionally tried to redirect the pupil in question, you have decided to engage in a closed choice strategy. You may choose to narrate this as follows:

'(Insert pupil name), it is disappointing that you are not engaging with the work that has been set. You now have two clear choices. You can either get on with the work set now or you will be removed from the lesson and you will have to complete the work during your lunch break. You now have 30 seconds to make a decision.'

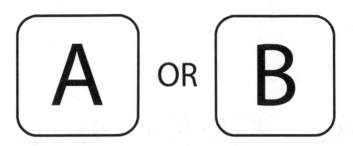

WARNING

If you are going to engage in a closed choice then you must be prepared to follow through with the option you ultimately would rather the pupil did not choose. Do not back down if the pupil fails to comply.

ADVICE

Closed choices make the refusal to complete the work set or to behave in a manner you expect a deliberate choice, which the pupil really cannot justify their position over.

PS

99: BRACKETING THE BEHAVIOUR

Bracketing the behaviour can be a really powerful and ultimately very subtle approach. You are presented, in your lesson, with a situation where four pupils are sat as a group. Three of the pupils are diligently getting on with the work and one pupil is making no effort at all to engage with the work that has been set. You could draw attention directly to the key pupil and potentially cause a scene within the lesson or you could employ the use of a more nuanced and subtle approach to spark the pupil into life.

NARRATING BRACKETING THE BEHAVIOUR

You have set your class off on an independent task. Four pupils are sat as a group, with three pupils fully engaged with the work. The fourth pupil has made no attempt to engage, to pick up their pen or to write anything and you are already five minutes into the task at hand. You may choose to narrate bracketing the behaviour as follows:

'Daisy, Matthew and Adele you are working beautifully and it is pleasing to see how much work you have produced so far. Well done, folks.'

The fourth pupil within this quartet is Sam. In bracketing the behaviour you have deliberately praised the work of three out of four of the pupils. You have deliberately made no reference to Sam and, in effect, ignored Sam. If this approach works successfully then Sam will realise he has been left out of your verbal praise and this will spark him into life.

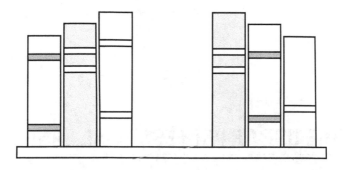

WARNING

Be prepared for bracketing the behaviour to potentially not work. Should this be the case, then you need to follow this up. A useful approach would be to look at Sam, as per the example above, and/or to walk over to Sam and look at his book over this shoulder.

ADVICE

This approach only works when you do not publicly reference the pupil whose behaviour you are trying to redirect. If you swiftly shift from bracketing the behaviour to then reprimanding the pupil you are trying to inadvertently focus on within the same breath, then this approach will have no impact.

PS

100: THE USE OF PROFESSIONAL LANGUAGE

Behaviour, and addressing behaviour, is hard. It can be hugely emotive at times. In certain situations, it is incredibly difficult to depersonalise a pupil's poor behavioural choices and not be affronted by them. A major issue is that teaching is not a job; it is a vocation. Teachers pour their hearts and souls into the preparation and delivery of their lessons. They invest inordinate amounts of time into what they do and take huge professional pride in how they perform and how effective they are. So, when a pupil derails a lesson, hinders the learning of others or deliberately antagonises or offends the teacher, it is hard not to take this personally. However, it is important to remember that we are the adults and that we have to behave as such. The use of the language that is employed when a pupil gets something wrong is crucial. If you select the wrong approach and become personal, you are likely to antagonise the pupil in question. Instead of addressing the behaviour that they have engaged with and de-escalating the matter, you could, inadvertently, make the situation worse.

HOW TO USE PROFESSIONAL LANGUAGE

Never become personal with the pupil. For example, do not use phrases such as 'You are an idiot.'	Always refer to the behaviour in question in the third person and pose questions. For example, 'Was that behaviour appropriate?'
In terms of the language employed, keep the dialogue with a pupil professional – as if you were talking to a colleague – and professionally adult in manner, tone and choice of phrase.	Link the language that you are using back to the school's expectations. For example, 'This is not how we behave at School X. You are not meeting the school's expectation. That is not School X.'

WARNING

At times it can be tempting to shout at a pupil. There is a real danger when you do this that you will have lost control of the situation. If you can feel yourself and your adrenaline bubbling up, then clam yourself before you engage with the pupil.

ADVICE

It would pay you to both script and rehearse how you will speak to a pupil so when you have to do it for real it is almost a case of pressing play.

PS

101: WORKING THE ROOM: YOUR POSITIONING IN RELATION TO THE PUPILS

How you utilise the space within your classroom is key to how you can manage behaviour, address issues and nip matters in the bud. There are a number of things you can do to support yourself in terms of how you work the room, as follows:

1. People will cite that different seating arrangements make a limited difference to lesson delivery. However, if your classroom is laid out in such a manner that pupils have to crane their heads, that they cannot see you or the board or that they are easily distracted because they are able to look at their friends then there is an issue. Furniture can play a big role in the success of your lessons. I would personally, in a secondary setting, have pupils in rows facing the teacher. Whatever furniture-based approach you take, you need to be confident that the whole class have their eyes on you when you are talking. Take, for example, primary phase teachers who bring the children down to the carpet. Why do they do this? So that they can have the undivided attention of the children on them. If you are to serve as the expert in the classroom then all eyes need to be on you when you are talking. It would be like going to the cinema and looking at the wall behind you. Your gaze is always forwards on the screen watching the film you have paid good money to see.

2. Once you engage the class in an independent task do not solely base yourself at the front of the room. One of the most powerful places to stand is at the back of the classroom. The pupils are never quite sure where you are and you can very easily and swiftly see if they are off-task or in need of your support. Standing here serves as one of your most powerful vantage points.

3. When a pupil goes off-task and you are fully aware that they are not engaging with the work that is set, then a powerful approach is to stand just behind them (but not too close) and look over their shoulder at the work that they should be doing. Without saying anything at all this approach can often trigger a pupil into action.

4. It is important that you both survey and work the room. Ensure that you move freely around your classroom so you can support pupils in a personalised manner but also so the pupils never quite know where you are.

5. When you are seeking to demonstrate something to your class, be it an art lesson, a PE lesson, a science practical, etc., you need to carefully consider how you pull the pupils safely together into an area of the room where you have their undivided attention. When you ask pupils to sit on the carpeted area (predominantly this will apply to primary) you need the children to know what the expectations are.

6. Sideways board writing. If you are the sort of teacher that likes to write on a whiteboard as you narrate, explain or model a problem to your class, then you need to consider how you stand at the board and simultaneously address the class and keep an eye on them. If you are continually writing on the board with your back to your class you may find that pupils begin to misbehave because ultimately you cannot see them. You need to practise (and it does take time to master) writing sideways on the board so you can see the class and the board simultaneously.

WARNING

Do not underestimate the importance of how your classroom is laid out. It can have a huge impact on the efficacy of your teaching and the learning.

ADVICE

Ensure that the focus and attention of the pupils is always firmly on you when you are speaking. If it is not, then you do not really have the attention of every pupil.

PS

102: SHOW ME YOUR BEST

Show me your best is a simple but effective classroom management approach that allows the teacher to command the attention of the class immediately. The idea of this approach is when a teacher says to their class 'show me your best' the pupils then respond by doing the following in one go:

- They sit upright.
- They fall silent.
- They put their pens/equipment down.
- They fold their arms.
- Their attention and focus are then on you as the teacher.

WARNING

You must train your pupils in how to do this and narrate the 'why' to them. This approach needs to become a habitual routine and one you have rehearsed with the pupils a lot for it to work. At no point should you compromise on any element of the process. So, for example, do not allow pupils to sit with their hands by their sides otherwise they will start to fiddle.

ADVICE

Do not employ this approach every 30 seconds. It has to serve a purpose and should be called upon at key points where you want the pupils to give you their undivided attention.

PS

103: VERBAL AND NON-VERBAL SIGNALS

Your use of voice, tone, body language and overall demeanour play a huge and vital role in your ability to manage a class. How you carry yourself, how confident you come across to your pupils and how you positively take charge and assert yourself over your class/classes can often make or break how you manage behaviour. The following set of verbal and non-verbal approaches will hopefully add another set of behavioural tools to your repertoire to draw on.

A: TIME PRESSURE

The use of time is an invaluable approach within lessons. Pupils not only need to know what is required of them when completing a task but also how long they have. As a teacher you need to be explicitly clear with how long any given task will take and what the expectations are of the pupils. It is also key that you stick clearly to the time allocation you have given to the class. As soon as you start to change your expectations, the pupils will quickly realise that your time parameters are elastic. You do not want to be in a position where pupils feel that the classroom boundaries and expectations that you have in place carry little meaning.

Time can also be used to add pace and impetus to the pupils. If you tell them they have five minutes left and then count this down every minute you can speed up the overall pace and increase the volume of work the pupils produce by adding in this layer of urgency.

B: STEADY STARE

This is a classic behaviour management strategy that is often taught on many teacher training behaviour workshops. When you have seen a pupil engaging in a behaviour you are not impressed with, that serves no purpose to support the learning or is distracting to others, then a clear, fixed, steady stare at the pupil in question can, at times, be enough for the pupil to have that moment of self-realisation and readjust their own behaviour accordingly.

C: USE OF VOICE

As a teacher, your voice, its use and its range are some of your most powerful tools. While all of us have a normal tone and pitch that we talk in most of the time, there are times where we need to change it up. You need to experiment trialling the range of your voice with your pupils to elicit key responses from them. For example, if you want to convey that you are not impressed you may choose to raise your voice. This is not to be confused with shouting, which is fundamentally different. Shouting is where your emotions have taken over. Raising your voice is for effect. You are in control of your emotions. You are raising it purely to demonstrate your displeasure and then reverting back to your normal tone.

You may wish to also try adding an excited, engaging tone when you really want to enthuse the pupils about something specific. With the same token, you may want to lower your voice to an almost quiet whisper when you want pupils to carefully listen to you.

D: BEING STERN

There will be times when you need to be explicitly stern. This works really well when you speak in a clear, assertive but simultaneously disappointed tone, utilising the words 'disappointed' and 'let down' to really emphasise your points. Building in deliberate moments of silence as you speak adds to the impact and effect of your stern approach.

E: NON-VERBAL SIGNALS

The use of your hands can have a real impact on redirecting pupil behaviour. For example, say a pupil is making no real effort to write anything or engage with the work. A strategy you could employ is to look at the pupil, point to the task on the board and make a writing gesture with your hand. This is to signal to the pupil that you know they are not doing any work and they need to. Another example is where a pupil is talking and should not be, you may try looking at the pupil in question and raising a finger to your mouth to signify that they should not be talking.

F: CONSISTENT AND CLEAR

It pays you to remain fully consistent and crystal clear with the use of language that you employ. The moment you add grey or uncertainty to your phrasing is when pupils will lack certainty regarding what they can and cannot do. For example, when you want the class to be silent and to listen to you: in this instance you do not want to ask the class to 'quieten down' or for there to be 'a little bit of quiet please'. Both of these phrases are meaningless. You need to give an instruction that is not open to interpretation or carries with it shades of grey. Pupils ultimately need total certainty regarding your expectations.

G: PRIVATE INTERVENTIONS

Sometimes it pays to speak to a pupil on their own to de-escalate a situation or to avoid platforming a problem to the rest of the class that could ultimately blow up in your face. You need to consider carefully when to publicly and when to privately engage with a pupil and you need to judge the situation and how they could respond very carefully. If you know that publicly platforming a pupil will create an adverse reaction, then why would you elect to do this? If you know that a quiet, private word outside the classroom or at the end of the lesson will have more impact, then choose to do this. You may find by privately speaking to the pupil you learn of a wider issue that needs to be addressed.

H: LISTENING

When you are addressing a pupil's poor behaviour it is often, though not necessarily always, worth asking a pupil why they have behaved in a certain manner. Once you ask a pupil 'Why did you behave that way?' listen carefully to their response. Sometimes, again not always, there may be an underlying reason as to why they have behaved in a certain manner, especially if the behaviour is uncharacteristic. Equally, if you are going to listen to a pupil then do not talk over them. If you start to talk over a pupil then they could respond negatively to this. Would you appreciate someone speaking over you?

I: THANK YOU, NOT PLEASE

When issuing an instruction or expectation to pupils finish your verbal instruction off with 'thank you'. While the use of 'please' is polite and courteous, you are ultimately changing the nature and tone of your instruction. Here are two examples that I will unpack:

Example 1:

'Please can you tuck your shirt in?'

The use of the word 'please' in this example turns the expectation from an assertive instruction into a form of pleading. You are, inadvertently, telling the pupil that you are appealing to their better self to do as you have asked. 'Please' is disempowering in this situation and undermines your position.

Example 2:

'Tuck your shirt in, thank you.'

In this example you have still been polite, courteous and professional. You have emphasised without any sense of ambiguity what the expectation is and the use of 'thank you' at the end transforms the narration of this expectation into one where the pupil is not being asked but told what to do.

J: USING SURNAMES

If you can, use surnames. By calling a pupil Mr Smith, Miss Jones, etc., you are conveying to them a sense that they are more adult and mature than their years suggest. Many pupils will see this as a sign of respect and it will make them feel a lot more grown up. Subliminally you are conveying to the pupils that you will treat them in a more adult fashion and address them as such if their behaviour mirrors your almost unwritten expectation.

K: MIRRORING

When a pupil is being very loud and perhaps lacks an awareness of just how loud they are being, mirror the behaviour back to make them aware. You could narrate this as follows:

'Mr Strickland, you are **BEING VERY LOUD AND TALKING LIKE THIS**.'

L: FEWER WORDS

Think carefully about how many words you will employ in a sentence. What will have the greater impact, a two-minute download or 10 carefully selected words? When you are dealing with behaviour keep the number of words you utilise to a minimum or you could lose the pupil you are trying to speak to.

M: PRECISE INSTRUCTIONS

When you are giving instructions, whatever they may be, ensure that your execution is precise, with no grey language used. Pupils need total clarity and certainty; they need to know exactly what you want them to do. If your instructions are not clear then do not be surprised if their response is muddled.

N: REMINDERS

It is really powerful to remind pupils of your expectations but to do so through the use of questions. For example, 'Pupil X, what is our rule about calling out?' This puts the onus on the pupil to address their own behavioural infringement.

O: PARTIAL AGREEMENTS

A pupil tells you that another member of staff lets them chew gum. Your partial agreement response should be framed as follows: 'Maybe teacher X does but in my lessons the expectations are clear, the bin is over there.' Do not get into a debate with the pupil about the other teacher.

P: TAKE-UP TIME

This is where you tactically give a pupil a small amount of time to action an expectation. An example could be where a pupil arrives late to your lesson. Rather than publicly address the lateness there and then you may choose, tactically, to direct the pupil to their seat and tell them to swiftly engage with what the rest of the class are doing. You should then carry on with the lesson but tactically, at a moment convenient to you, speak with the pupil in question to both ascertain why they are late and direct them to the work you are completing as a class.

Q: BEHAVIOURAL REDIRECTION

This is where you refer to a pupil directly but cite the behaviour you want to see as opposed to the behaviour you do not want to see. For example, 'Sam, face this way, stop talking and listen to me, thank you.' This is more powerful than 'Do not talk when I am talking, Sam.'

R: DIRECT QUESTIONS

Try and consider framing your questions to pupils around 'What?', 'When?' and 'How?'

S: DIRECT CHOICES

This is when you are clear with a pupil about what they can do. For example, 'You can type up your essay once you have completed your draft on paper and I have checked it.'

WARNING

Avoid shouting at pupils. As much as you may think that this will have a positive impact on pupils it is likely to have the reverse effect. You are more likely to elicit a negative response from a pupil who feels threatened by what can be perceived as irrational behaviour. This could manifest into a parental complaint about your professionalism, with a parent citing that you are intimidatory in your approach. Equally, pupils may become immune to you shouting all the time and feel it makes you look rather silly, which can undermine you.

ADVICE

All of the strategies detailed in this section must be rehearsed and ideally role-played/practised before you use them. They will also take time and experience to judge when best to employ their use. You also need to accept that you may well get the approach wrong or that its execution may not land in the way that you had hoped.

104: THINK-PAIR-SHARE

Think-Pair-Share is a superb co-operative learning approach where a class is given a question or prompt to discuss. Pupils first consider the question/prompt on their own, then they form pairs to discuss their thoughts and then they engage in a wider whole-class discussion. This approach promotes oracy within the enacted curriculum, builds pupil confidence, supports the retention of knowledge and importantly supports pupils in the application of knowledge. It is a great strategy to build pupil focus, attention and engagement.

HOW TO IMPLEMENT THIS APPROACH

Think-Pair-Share should be utilised as a retrieval approach, allowing a low-stakes, low-risk opportunity for pupils to formulate their responses to a question/prompt before sharing them widely.	As a teacher you need to carefully consider how open-ended your question/prompt is and also think about where pupils may stumble into misconceptions.
The teacher should carefully narrate this approach and how it works to the class, employing the use of clear guidelines and timings at each step.	Once the pupils are ready to share their feedback and ideas you need to decide how you will question them and ensure that everyone participates.

WARNING

Before engaging in an activity like this, you need to ascertain how secure the pupils' subject knowledge is. If it is not secure then this strategy will not work and pupils will struggle to adeptly engage with it.

ADVICE

Consider carefully how you, and more importantly the pupils, will capture the learning in their books following the use of this strategy, otherwise the learning may be lost.

PS

105: ARTICULATING FULL SENTENCES

Some people will cite that insisting pupils articulate themselves in full sentences, especially when they are offering answers in a lesson, is artificial. That it does not reflect how adults speak when conversing with one another and that speaking in such a manner is clumsy. I would refute this. When pupils are encouraged to speak in full sentences, offering a full answer, it promotes them to think hard about what they are going to say. Pupils will pause, will consider what is being taught and will want to speak fully and in an articulate manner, especially if this is the established classroom norm. Educationally it has huge benefits. With pupils honing their oratorical skills they become more engaged with the learning, they want to show off their ability to speak, they want to demonstrate their knowledge and, importantly, if pupils understand how to articulate themselves fully, then there will be direct benefits to their written work. This approach comes under the banner of high expectations. With high expectations come improved behaviour and attitudes to learning. Clearly this is an approach that can only be actioned once a child has developed their speech and the ability to speak in full sentences.

The following demonstrates how a full sentence response can work:

Example 1:
Question: 'When did the First World War end?'

Answer: '1918.'

In this example the answer is correct but lacks subject specificity and is actually quite a lazy answer.

Example 2:
Question: 'When did the First World War end?'

Answer: 'The First World War ended at 11am on the 11th November 1918, Mr Strickland.'

In this example the pupil is giving a full and factually detailed answer and is addressing this to the teacher.

WARNING

You need to model and rehearse how to verbally answer questions fully to your pupils and do so regularly or they will not understand how to do it.

ADVICE

When pupils give you an answer play games with it. For example, ask them to say their answer more clearly, more loudly. Ask other pupils to repeat the answer, especially if it is a powerful piece of knowledge you want everyone to know. Get the whole class to repeat it. The more pupils articulate something verbally, the more likely they are to remember it.

106: DE-ESCALATING ISSUES

There are some children who find school challenging and they do carry with them social, emotional and mental health needs that require reasonable adjustments to be put into place to support them throughout their time in school. I personally do not believe we should lower our expectations, but instead we should support these children to meet our expectations. De-escalation is where we try to calm a situation with a pupil before it adversely erupts.

WHEN SHOULD WE DE-ESCALATE?

There are often a number of signals that indicate a pupil may become aggressive or lose control. They tend to become highly agitated, they fidget, shake, clench their jaw, clench their fists, and become more high-pitched in their tone and more challenging. Their behaviour borders on irrational.

HOW TO DE-ESCALATE

You need to maintain a clear, calm and measured tone of voice. You also need to adopt and employ the use of respectful and polite language towards the pupil. It is also best to stand at a distance from the pupil in question and avoid invading their personal space. As a member of staff you should adopt a neutral facial expression, control your own breathing so it is regular and calm, and lower your voice, with a calm even tone.

POINTS TO NOTE

When a pupil becomes more challenging and aggressive, they are often responding with their flight or fight instincts. They are not thinking about their own actions nor the consequences of those actions. Try and distract the pupil and their thinking by asking them what may appear to be a random question. For example, a question about the weather, their favourite food, their favourite film, etc. You also need to give the pupil a multitude of choices as opposed to a set of closed choices when you are trying to redirect their behaviour.

KEY ADVICE

Do not get drawn into secondary behaviours such as arguing back. Arguing back is a defence mechanism to deflect, upset and/or get rid of you. Always acknowledge the child's feelings and praise them when they tell you something. Acknowledge how difficult the situation must be for them.

PHRASES TO USE

Try and adopt broad and open phrases, for example:

'Let's try...'

'Maybe we can...'

'It seems as if...'

It is also important that you do not engage in an argument with the pupil. If you want a pupil to sit down, for example, then you need to calmly remind them that you want them to sit down. Don't retort to the pupil with 'You are not doing as I have said.' Do say 'X, I need you to sit down for me please.' Also, give the pupil what I would refer to as 'take-up time' to process your direction and allow them to consider it slowly.

THINGS TO AVOID

It is key that you avoid threatening a pupil with sanctions in this situation. This will not help. You should also avoid being defensive or taking anything that may be said by the pupil personally. Ultimately, the level of aggression being displayed by the pupil in this situation is not about you. Avoid sarcasm and humour at all costs. This will further antagonise the situation.

WARNING

It is important to note that irrespective of how carefully and skilfully you attempt to de-escalate a situation, it may still reach a crisis point. Try to find an opportune moment when dealing with a situation that needs de-escalating to alert another member of staff so they are able to support you if necessary.

ADVICE

Following an outburst by a pupil where a situation needs to be de-escalated, it is important to remember that the sanctions applied are appropriate and proportionate to the behaviour. This should not be seen as an opportunity to seek redemption. The most important factor is the certainty with which the behaviour has been challenged rather than the severity. It is also important that there is a follow-up with the pupil to review what happened and to learn from any mistakes that have been made.

PS

107: ENDING LESSONS

How you end a lesson is just as important as how you start it. Do you just close the lid on the lesson and dismiss the class, or do you have a clear and orderly routine for how you do this? Some colleagues like to use exit tickets, which can be an impactful way of ascertaining what pupils have/ have not learned that lesson. Some staff like to ask the class for one thing that they have learned today. My own view is that you should revisit the key pieces of powerful knowledge that you wanted the class to learn that lesson. The following is an example of how you could end a lesson.

AN EXAMPLE OF HOW TO END A LESSON

- Instruct the class to pass their workbooks/exercise books to the end of their row – *this allows the exercise books/workbooks to be swiftly collected in.*

- Instruct the class to tidy up their belongings – *this ensures that they are packed away and ready to move to their next lesson.*

- Instruct the class to stand up behind their desks and push their chairs in – *in effect this is tidying the room for you, with the room being left ready for the next class.*

- Walk with a bin around the room and ask pupils to pick up any litter and place it in the bin – *in doing this you are keeping your room regularly tidy.*

- As you walk the room, survey the pupils to ensure they are wearing their uniform correctly – *this supports the school's approach to uniform, expectations and standards.*

- As you walk the room, ask the class to chorally repeat the key powerful knowledge that you have presented and taught that lesson – *this further encourages the pupils to verbally articulate the knowledge that you need them to remember.*
- When you are satisfied, dismiss the class a row at a time – *this allows you to dismiss the class in an orderly fashion.*

WARNING

If your lesson ending is chaotic pupils are likely to then move on to their next lesson in the wrong frame of mind. You are effectively making things more difficult for your colleagues.

ADVICE

It is important that you give the end of your lesson careful thought and that there is no dead/lost learning time in your lessons.

108: REBOOTS

At times you will need to reboot your behavioural expectations. The reality is pupils will match your expectations brilliantly one lesson, leaving you thinking that you have cracked it, and then the next lesson they will forget some of the basics. It is important that you never take this personally. In equal measure, avoid taking your frustration out on your class. You must, at all times, maintain your professional cool, so to speak, but it is okay to voice disappointment when your expectations are not being lived up to.

REBOOT CONSIDERATIONS

1. Capping a lesson.
If you have a lesson where things are not going to plan, you may wish to put a lid on the lesson and cap the activities that you have planned. For example, the pupils may not be adhering to your expectations or an activity/approach has fallen flat on its face. It is not a sign of weakness to say to a class to put the activity to one side or to totally change tack and have the class copy out of a textbook in silence for a period of time so you can regain control of the group.

2. Growing trends.
You may have noticed over a series of lessons that there is a growing trend of poor behaviour. You need to put a lid on this and reboot your expectations with the class.

3. Pre-emptive reboots.

Following a holiday or if you are going to fully change tack in how your lessons are delivered, you may wish to build in tactical reboots so you are continuously reminding your pupils of your expectations, routines and norms.

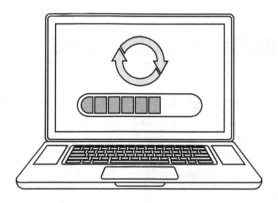

WARNING

If poor behaviour begins to creep into your lessons and you do not address it with a reboot of your expectations, then the situation will invariably get worse.

ADVICE

Rebooting pupil behaviour, especially if the reboots are part of a planned and sequenced approach, is critical to maintaining an effective approach and should form part of your overall routine lesson delivery.

PS

109: CURRICULUM APPROACHES

This book is not strictly speaking a curriculum book, but behaviour is and should be part of the curriculum as a whole. The way in which we order, sequence and deliver our curriculum is key. I wanted to share two models of curriculum design with you, purely for you to consider the enacted delivery of your approach and how this can positively support pupil behaviour.

MODEL 1: RON BERGER'S *AN ETHIC OF EXCELLENCE*[15]

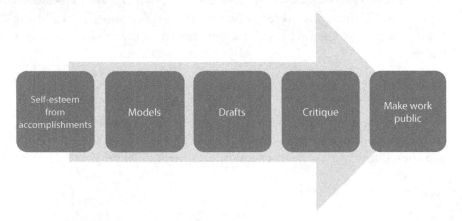

This model is built on platforming and celebrating pupil work and raising the overall self-esteem of your pupils.

MODEL 2: ROSENSHINE[16]

1: Presenting new material using small steps	6: Guide student practice
2: Provide models	7: Obtain a high success rate
3: Provide scaffolds for difficult tasks	8: Independent practice
4: Ask questions	9: Daily review
5: Check student understanding	10: Weekly and monthly review

A lot has been written on the value and importance of Rosenshine's Principles as a model and I would encourage you to read up on this.

WARNING

It is important to ensure that you both model and scaffold the learning in your lessons or pupils will simply not understand how to do it.

ADVICE

You should consider carefully how you will praise pupils. Some pupils thrive on public platforming; others prefer to be spoken to more subtly. Knowing your pupils is key.

PS

110: PARENTAL ENGAGEMENT

Whether you are a class teacher or a form tutor, it is really important that you forge and foster a professional working relationship with the parents of the children you teach. Parents ultimately play a crucial role in supporting their child's learning and there is extensive research that shows the more parents are involved, the better the academic outcomes of their child. I do appreciate that there is also little training on this matter and the mothership should really consider what and how it would like you to communicate with home.

SOME KEY IDEAS

Send a welcome email to the parents of your tutor group/classes outlining who you are and your role for the academic year in question.	Communicate your curriculum, homework tasks, suggested reading and how parents can support their child at home well in advance.
Create a summary video that outlines how parents can support their child at home.	Send bespoke and tailored communications to families that celebrate their child's successes, with positive messaging about their progress and learning.

WARNING

Getting the right balance with your parental communication and accessibility is critical. You do not want to be in a position where all you are doing is fielding parental calls. That said, where there is an issue, contact home before the pupil goes home and offers a warped version of events.

ADVICE

At the start of any new academic year or when you pick up a new class, it is best to get in early with parents and proactively introduce yourself and your expectations. You should always present your communications positively and from a stance of offering support.

S

111: THE IMPORTANCE OF BEING A FORM TUTOR

In many schools there is heavy emphasis on the role that the form tutor plays, and they are integral to the way in which a school operates. From your perspective as a teacher you have to straddle two domains, namely academic and pastoral. Throughout my own career there has been very little training given in how to be a tutor and how this vital role works. Tutors often spend 15 to 20 minutes a day with their tutees in a secondary setting, whereas in a primary setting you essentially have to perform a pastoral role at any moment in the day. Tutors perform a number of vital roles: they are listeners, problem solvers, they manage behaviour, they help motivate their tutees, they can be asked to monitor academic progress and they are often the first point of contact for parents. In many regards, they are the in-school parent for their tutor group.

KEY POINTS TO CONSIDER

Pupils will look to you as their primary point of contact. It is important that you build a swift and positive set of relationships with the pupils.	You should carefully consider – especially if tutor time is not planned for you centrally – the structure of your tutor time sessions and the content that you will deliver.
Routines are critical and, as much as your lessons will require routines for learning, so will your tutor times.	Making contact, especially early on in your time as the tutor, to establish a rapport with families is key. You need to gain their faith and trust as much as you need to build relationships with your tutees.

WARNING

If you adopt a frame of mind that tutor time is just 15 to 20 minutes a day to kill, so will your pupils. Your tutor times will, at worst, descend into chaos. This is ultimately a huge waste of institutional time, your time and the pupils' time.

ADVICE

Your tutor time sessions should be purposeful and pupils should come away from each session further enriched educationally. Ideally your tutor periods should be structured like a mini lesson and link clearly to the school's values.

PS

112: DEALING WITH EMERGENCIES

Sadly, at some stage you are going to have to respond to an emergency situation. It is important to think through how you would deal with an emergency, and it is certainly worthwhile speaking with your line manager to discuss how to deal with emergency situations. All schools worth their salt will give their staff a handbook. Within the handbook there should be a section on dealing with emergency situations and first aid matters. I am going outline four key areas that may come your way.

KEY SITUATIONS

Requesting support: You need to familiarise yourself, before you even teach a class, with the school's on-call system. Many schools will operate a system whereby a more senior member of staff will come to support you if a pupil needs to be removed, as an example.	**A violent situation:** It is possible that you will have a pupil who erupts in a lesson and becomes physically violent or displays the potential risk that they may become violent. In this situation you need to alert someone to support you and to swiftly remove the rest of the class from the situation, leaving the pupil in question in the classroom you were teaching in. In essence, you are isolating the issue to safeguard the rest of the class until support arrives.
First aid: This can cause any teacher real anxiety and worry when a first aid issue presents itself. It is important that you know what your school's first aid protocols are and action them swiftly if there is an issue. It is also important to move your class away from the situation and, if need be, send a reliable pupil to seek assistance.	**Sickness:** You are likely to encounter a pupil who does not feel well. This can, at times, present challenging judgement calls regarding whether you send them home or not. Many schools have a system in place for this, which again you should familiarise yourself with.

WARNING

If you do not familiarise yourself with your school's protocols and systems for dealing with emergencies, you will come unstuck.

ADVICE

You need to take the view that there are no stupid questions when considering how you will deal with emergencies. Always speak to a line manager or senior leader when you are not sure how a process or system works.

PS

113: SAFEGUARDING

For many staff, especially less experienced staff, safeguarding is an area that can cause a lot of anxiety. This singular area is vast. It ranges from radicalisation, to CSE, to domestic violence, to FGM, to gangs and so on and so on. It is a curriculum in its own right. Staff are expected to know about safeguarding and they have a professional responsibility to safeguard the children in their care. Schools should provide all staff with annual safeguarding Level 1 training and ideally regular safeguarding updates. It is also best practice to engage in annual Prevent and anti-radicalisation training. Teachers are expected to keep an eye out for safeguarding concerns and respond accordingly. The reality is that every child is everyone's responsibility and every child is potentially vulnerable.

SAFEGUARDING HINTS/TIPS

There are four key categories of abuse to look out for: **Physical** (for example, FGM, bruising, scalding), **emotional** (for example, treatment that causes adverse effects on a child's emotional development), **sexual** (for example, enticing a minor to take part in sexual activities, but can include non-contact activities such as grooming) and **neglect** (for example, a persistent failure to meet a child's basic needs).	Your role as a teacher is to recognise and respond to a safeguarding matter. In other words, you should look out for the signs of a safeguarding concern and your response should be to refer it to the school's DSL (Designated Safeguarding Lead). It is not for you to investigate nor attempt to resolve the matter at hand.
If a child makes a disclosure to you do not promise at any stage you will keep the matter to yourself.	Always keep an accurate, factual and non-opinionated log of any disclosure that you take.

WARNING

Sometimes a safeguarding matter can really impact on a teacher. Should you find yourself in a position where you are personally affected, then talk to someone more senior within your school setting for support.

ADVICE

Consider carefully your own working practice to ensure that you keep yourself safe at all times. Do not put yourself in a position where someone could make a false allegation about you. Professional boundaries with children are key. Always stand where you can be seen by others, ideally in a room with a door open and where you are not obstructing the exit for the pupil so you cannot be accused of blocking their path.

PS

114: EDUCATIONAL VISITS

Educational visits are fantastic and can really serve to enhance and enrich the curriculum and the educational experience pupils receive. They can take on many guises, ranging from a trip to the local woods, to observing differing elements of the town most local to your school, to a trip to a museum, gallery or theatre, or, further afield, an overnight residential or a trip abroad. In my own experience, I have either been involved in or have directly organised almost every type of trip you can imagine. If you want your trip to be successful then you need to be crystal clear with families, pupils and staff of the expectations that you have in place. Before you embark on planning a trip, always liaise with your school's EVC and ensure that all of your risk assessments specifically reference pupil behaviour.

POINTS TO CONSIDER

Do the expectations of your trip/visit marry up with the school's expectations? Have you spoken to the member of staff that is directly responsible for trips and visits about what the rules, sanctions and expectations are of pupils when on a school trip?	Send home a letter, an agreement form and, ideally, a video that details what the expectations and parameters of your educational trip are. Parents, when giving their consent, must sign a document that details that they agree to the expectations you have laid out.
Hold a briefing session for the pupils you are taking on the trip. If the trip is a residential then I would recommend parents are in attendance. During this briefing you need to be explicitly clear about the expectations that you have in place.	Ensure that you have taken the time to brief any accompanying staff who are supporting you on your trip and that you minute your briefing. If you have organised a residential trip then you must host a daily briefing that is recorded.

WARNING

Trips are hugely rewarding but equally tiring. Do not assume that pupils or staff will know how to behave on a trip. You have to be explicitly clear on your dos and do nots. You must keep firmly in mind that you are in loco parentis, especially as a trip lead.

ADVICE

It is always worthwhile producing a small, business-style laminated card that has your trip expectations and the key contact numbers of staff members on the trip (those numbers should be school mobile phone numbers not your personal ones). You should issue this to both pupils and staff alike and on the day of the trip rehearse these expectations again. Whatever you want or expect to see happen on your trip, you have to be explicitly clear.

PS

115: YOU: THE HALLMARKS OF AN EFFECTIVE TEACHER

Whether you believe it or not, you are critical in supporting school improvement and generating the right culture, climate and ethos within the school that you work in. The collective efforts of all the staff combined make a school, with expert leadership setting the rhythm and beat of the strategy at play. But you, as the class teacher, are key. 70-80% of any given school's budget is on staffing. You are the mothership's most prized entity. While the mothership has a professional and moral duty to look after you, you also need to consider your own self-preservation. Teaching five to six hours a day back-to-back takes its toll. People hugely underestimate the energy levels that are required. You have to adopt the mindset that your job is akin to a marathon and not a sprint. If you go too fast and too hard at it too soon into a term, you will be burnt out before you hit the midway point of any half-term.

The reality is you are vital to how your classroom operates day in and day out. If you are exhausted or teaching with an intense headache then you will be nowhere near as effective as when you are fresh at the start of a term. If we think of it in a sporting sense, you cannot expect an athlete to perform at the same level of high intensity and with the same level of efficacy as if they were playing their respective sport for six hours straight, five days a week. Once you hit your own version of the runner's wall, your classroom management will slip. Pupils who look for a chink in your armour often sense when you are not quite on it.

Another area to consider is your own personal organisation and how you prepare yourself for the working week ahead and your lessons. This all has a bearing on how you teach and, as per the theme of this book, the behaviour of the pupils.

What I want to share with you in this section are some of the hallmarks of an effective teacher and some of the things that often no one tells you to have in place for your working week.

PERSONAL ORGANISATION

Buy a cloth-style toolbox from a hardware store to carry all of your key items in when at work. This may sound silly but you almost need your own teacher toolkit.	Ensure you have several board pens, a class set of biros (to lend to pupils), a four-colour Bic pen for yourself, a ruler, a board rubber, hand gel, a box of tissues and a printed set of class registers for the classes you teach.
Always have a pack of Nurofen and paracetamol to hand. You never know when you may develop a headache.	Ensure you have plenty of water on your person to drink, but the warning shot is then needing to go to the toilet, which is extremely tricky when you are in full-flow teaching.
A complete change of clothes, including underwear and hosiery is essential – ultimately you never know when an accident can happen and you need to change your attire.	A whistle – this is key if you teach PE but also an essential if you are on duty, especially on the playground.
A bag of toiletries, which includes deodorant, mouthwash, a spray and sanitary products. You may need to freshen up at some stage in the school day, especially if you are backing into a long parent consultation evening.	Fruit/a protein or chocolate bar – it is really important to have a mini stash of filling quick bites. Time is a premium in schools and all too often a sit-down lunch is a luxury.
A spare HDMI cable and a remote clicker – you just never know when technology will fail on you. A clicker is essential if you use PowerPoint.	A back-up bank of 3-4 lessons – if your teaching is reliant on technology then what do you do If the technology fails you? Have a few aces up your sleeve to swiftly shift your lesson modus operandi so pupils do not become restless while you are waiting for IT support to fix your laptop.

CLASSROOM ORGANISATION

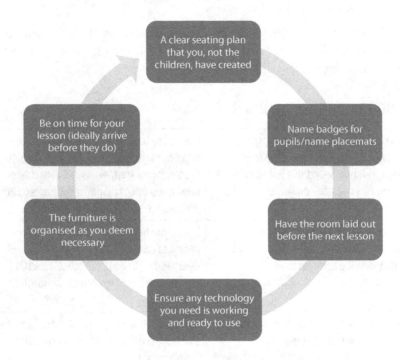

COMMON HALLMARKS OF AN EFFECTIVE TEACHER

- They are personally prepared.
- They are prepared for their lessons, with the right equipment.
- They arrive on time to their own classes.
- They organise and teach their pupils clear routines.
- They meet and greet pupils on arrival.
- They use praise proportionately and effectively *but* not cheaply.
- They learn the names of the pupils.
- They can effectively use non-verbal cues to get the attention of the class but this comes with experience and practice.
- They can survey their room and spot issues.
- They use positive language.

- They adhere to and uphold the school's rules.
- They depersonalise poor behaviour, separating it from the individual.
- They know when to tactically ignore issues but follow up in a timely manner.
- They are not frightened to reboot behaviour when necessary.
- They have clear routines for tidying their room, that utilise the pupils so the whole onus does not fully fall on the teacher.

WARNING

The list above is by no means exhaustive. The reality is that an effective teacher is a master plate spinner, having to make hundreds of decisions every single lesson. This will sound hugely daunting but, as with any routine, once it becomes habitual it will just become part of your established norm.

ADVICE

All of these key hallmarks will help you to ensure the conditions for positive behaviour are there. You should be mindful that they may not guarantee positive behaviour and there will be times when a pupil misbehaves. It is important to keep this in perspective and never blame yourself.

116: OFSTED QUESTIONS

As a teaching member of staff you will potentially be asked questions by Ofsted about behaviour in your school. The following is an outline of the type of questions you could be asked.

EXAMPLE QUESTIONS

- Can you define the school's culture for me?
- Do you think the school has improved since it was last inspected? If so, how and why?
- Are pupils safe at this school? If not, why?
- Do staff consistently manage behaviour well?
- Is behaviour at least good?
- Do leaders support you with behaviour?
- What are the systems and processes that have been put in place by the school?
- Do you receive training in how to manage and respond to poor behaviour? Elaborate.
- How does the school deal with bullying? Is bullying common?
- How are attendance and punctuality chased up?
- Are pupils respectful to one another?
- What educational support do the pupils receive when issues such as bullying, homophobia and racism emerge?

- Do pupils feel confident to discuss and debate issues where they present their own views?
- Are there high expectations for all?
- How are the needs of SEND pupils met?

THE MICRO LEVEL: CONCLUDING THOUGHTS

'If you have to put someone on a pedestal, put teachers. They are society's heroes.' Guy Kawasaki[17]

The role of a teacher is multifaceted. They possess incredible nurturing skills coupled with razor-sharp subject knowledge. Teachers, the very best teachers, really care about the children that they serve but equally know a lot of 'stuff'. They instil immense belief into their pupils that they can achieve anything and that nothing is impossible. In equal measure, the children believe in them. Building such relationships is not easy. They take time and patience and, as I have identified in this section of the book multiple times, lots and lots of scripting and rehearsing. Teachers have to perform a thousand different functions every single lesson, all at speed and with grace, agility and precision. A primary-phase teacher has the marathon slog of the same 30 children in front of them all day, every day. Conversely, the secondary-phase teacher has the conveyor belt syndrome, with a changing audience every hour. An audience that they may not see until the end of the week. They also have an array of year groups to teach, with varying demands. Both situations can be tough and exhausting gigs.

The more you can do to plan, script and rehearse your systems, routines, norms and behavioural expectations – so they are habitual for you – the better. These key approaches are as important as your subject knowledge, curriculum design and lesson planning. If, indeed, not more so, because if the behaviour in your classroom is not right then everything you try and do will be built on sand.

KEY TAKEAWAY POINTS

1. You should know precisely what culture you want within your own classroom setting.
2. You need to consider carefully how to communicate your cultural and behavioural expectations to the pupils you teach.
3. You need to teach your routines, classroom expectations and norms until they become habitual.
4. Relationships are critical to your success as a teacher.
5. Always nip issues swiftly in the bud.
6. There are ultimately no tricks, no gimmicks and no silver bullets when it comes to behaviour, just lots of hard work.

COMMON MISCONCEPTIONS

1. Routines suffocate your freedom and creativity as a teacher.
2. Good lesson planning automatically results in good pupil behaviour.
3. Pupils should automatically know how to behave without ever being shown and trained.
4. Methods of deliberate practice are Victorian in nature.
5. Poor behaviour is the teacher's fault.

REFLECTIONS

Please use the following space, having read the teacher/micro level section, to write any key reflections or take-home points that you are considering or may action.

CONCLUDING COMMENTS

FINAL REMARKS

This book should have given you a lot of food for thought. It may have reinforced your thinking. It may have opened up your mind to a new way of considering how to support behaviour. It may have added to your armoury of strategies to call upon to drive behaviour or it may have supported your toolkit with approaches that you had not considered. Either way, I hope it has served to help you. The journey to supporting positive behaviour in schools is not an easy one. It requires hard work, relentless determination and consistent follow-through. If there was a magic silver bullet that ensured all pupils behaved in the precise manner that we wanted, and when we wanted, then life would be so much easier for us all and this book would be obsolete.

It is important to remember that when pupils misbehave it is often not the teacher's fault. Far too many teachers in far too many schools are the victims of poor behaviour and this ultimately undermines their ability to deliver the curriculum, to be effective and, crucially, to enjoy their job. Their own halcyon dream can be swiftly crushed by unruly pupils who continue to misbehave in their lessons. It is also important to remember that all schools at some stage encounter behavioural issues. Even the glowing Ofsted Outstanding schools (and I have worked in three) have their problems. How senior leaders, middle leaders, teachers and all other staff work together as one collective unit will make or break a school. If we adopt a philosophy of collective security in our schools then all staff, at all levels, will feel supported, valued and cared for.

What this book should have offered you is a series of proactive steps and tools that you can action, irrespective of your position within a school, to lay down the foundations and parameters for good behaviour. This front-footed bedrock will serve you well. It won't resolve every single issue and there will, at times, be a need to respond to events as they arise. But the more proactive we are in our systems, approaches and thinking, the more we can pre-empt issues and support pupils to make the right decisions. It is important to be clear that the approaches I have discussed and presented in this book are not about doing things to children, but about enabling them to be free to learn, to thrive and to succeed.

School improvement and supporting positive behaviour requires resilience. There are no tricks, no gimmicks. To think that there are is a fool's gold. Poor behaviour is kryptonite to all that we are trying to achieve.

Spero!

Sam Strickland

REFLECTIONS

Please use the following space, having read this book, to write any key reflections or take-home points that you are considering or may action.

_____

_____

_____

_____

_____

_____

_____

_____

_____

_____

_____

_____

_____

_____

_____

_____

_____

_____

REFERENCES

1: Peterson, J. quoted in Bhatt, A. (2021) *90 best Jordan Peterson quotes (author of 12 rules for life).* Available at: https://bit.ly/3vAN2PK (Accessed: 23 February 2022).

2: Lemov, D. (2010) *Teach like a champion.* San Francisco, CA: Jossey-Bass.

3: Fulton, J. *How important is consistency in behaviour management?* Available at: https://bit.ly/3DGHPbg (Accessed: 23 February 2022).

4: Blatchford, R. (2014) *The restless school.* Woodbridge: John Catt Educational.

5: Covey, S. (1999) *The 7 habits of highly effective people.* London: Simon & Schuster UK.

6: Sinek, S. (2020) *Find your why.* Available at: https://simonsinek.com/find-your-why/ (Accessed: 7 March 2022).

7: Carter, R. quoted in Goldin, K. (2018) *Great leaders take people where they may not want to go.* Available at: https://bit.ly/3MkofoZ (Accessed: 4 March 2022).

8: Rosenthal, R. (2003) *Pygmalion in the classroom.* Wales: Crown House Publishing Limited.

9: Wiliam, D. quoted in Still, K. (2017) *The single most important thing for teachers to know.* Available at: https://bit.ly/35nAxwp (Accessed: 4 March 2022).

10: Lemov, D. (2010) *Teach like a champion*. San Francisco, CA: Jossey-Bass.

11: Rogers, B. quoted in Sherrington, T. (2019) *Behaviour management: A Bill Rogers top 10*. Available at: www.learningsciences.com/blog/behaviour-management-a-bill-rogers-top-10/ (Accessed: 4 March 2022).

12: Marzano, R. quoted in Resilient Educator. (2020) *Overview of Robert Marzano's model of teaching effectiveness*. Available at: https://bit.ly/3pFQOn5 (Accessed: 4 March 2022).

13: Lemov, D. (2010) *Teach like a champion*. San Francisco, CA: Jossey-Bass.

14: Lemov, D. (2010) *Teach like a champion*. San Francisco, CA: Jossey-Bass.

15: Berger, R. (2003) *An ethic of excellence: Building a culture of craftsmanship with students*. US: Heinemann Educational Books.

16: Rosenshine, B. (2012) *Principles of instruction: Research-based strategies that all teachers should know*. Available at: www.teachertoolkit.co.uk/wp-content/uploads/2018/10/Principles-of-Insruction-Rosenshine.pdf (Accessed: 7 March 2022).

17: Kawasaki, G. (n. d.) *Guy Kawasaki quotes*. Available at: www.brainyquote.com/quotes/guy_kawasaki_458310 (Accessed: 7 March 2022).

'The moment you doubt whether you can fly, you cease forever to be able to do it.'

Peter Pan

9 781915 261243